3rd Workshop on Semantic Deep Learning 2018 (SemDeep-3)

Santa Fe, New Mexico, USA
20 August 2018

ISBN: 978-1-5108-6911-0

Printed from e-media with permission by:

Curran Associates, Inc.
57 Morehouse Lane
Red Hook, NY 12571

Some format issues inherent in the e-media version may also appear in this print version.

Printed by Curran Associates, Inc. (2018)

Association for Computational Linguistics
209 N. Eighth Street
Stroudsburg, Pennsylvania 18360

Phone: 1-570-476-8006
Fax: 1-570-476-0860

acl@aclweb.org

Additional copies of this publication are available from:

Curran Associates, Inc.
57 Morehouse Lane
Red Hook, NY 12571 USA
Phone: 845-758-0400
Fax: 845-758-2633
Email: curran@proceedings.com
Web: www.proceedings.com

COLING 2018

The Third Workshop on Semantic Deep Learning (SemDeep-3)

Proceedings

August 20th, 2018
Santa Fe, New Mexico, USA

Preface

This third workshop on Semantic Deep Learning (SemDeep-3) invited researchers and professionals in computational linguistics to report results and systems on the possible contributions of Deep Learning to classical problems in semantic applications, such as meaning representation, dependency parsing, semantic role labeling, word sense disambiguation, semantic relations extraction, statistical relation learning, knowledge base completion, or semantically grounded inferences.

There are notable examples of contributions leveraging either deep neural architectures or distributed representations learned via deep neural networks in the broad area of Semantic Web technologies, such as ontology learning or prediction. Ontologies, on the other hand, have been repeatedly utilized as background knowledge for machine learning tasks. This interplay between structured knowledge and corpus-based approaches has given way to knowledge- rich embeddings, which in turn have proven useful for tasks such as hypernym discovery, collocation discovery and classification, word sense disambiguation, and many others.

This workshop consists of five papers with oral presentations (three of which also present a poster in a joint session) and two invited talks. Steven Schockaert from Cardiff University gives an invited talk entitled "Knowledge Representation with Conceptual Spaces", which will focus on learning Gärdenfors' conceptual spaces as an alternative to entity embeddings. Christos Christodoulopoulos from Amazon Research Cambridge talks about "Knowledge Representation and Extraction at Scale", which will detail methods for building and maintaining a knowledge base for Alexa as well as fact extraction and verification techniques.

Organizing Committee

Luis Espinosa Anke, Cardiff University, UK
Thierry Declerck, German Research Centre for Artificial Intelligence (DFKI GmbH), Saarbrücken, Germany
Dagmar Gromann, Technical University Dresden (TU Dresden), Dresden, Germany

Keynote Speakers

Steven Schockaert, Cardiff University, UK
Christos Christodoulopoulos, Amazon Research Cambridge, UK

Programme Committee

Kemo Adrian, Artificial Intelligence Research Institute (IIIA-CSIC), Bellaterra, Spain
Luu Ahn Tuan, Institute for Infocomm Research, Singapore
Miguel Ballesteros, IBM T.J. Watson Research Center, Yorktown Heights, NY, USA
Jose Camacho-Collados, Sapienza University of Rome, Rome, Italy
Eugenio Martínez Cámara, University of Granada, Spain
Gerard Casamayor, Pompeu Fabra University, Spain
Maarten Grachten, Austrian Research Institute for AI, Vienna, Austria
Dario Garcia-Casulla, Barcelona Supercomputing Center (BSC), Barcelona, Spain
Jorge Gracia Del Río, Ontology Engineering Group, UPM, Spain
Jindrich Helcl, Charles University, Prague, Czech Republic
Petya Osenova, Bulgarian Academy of Sciences, Sofia, Bulgaria
Martin Riedl, Hamburg University, Germany Stephen Roller, Facebook AI Research
Francesco Ronzano, Pompeu Fabra University, Barcelona, Spain
Enrico Santus, The Hong Kong Polytechnic University, Hong Kong
Francois Scharffe, Axon Research, New York, USA
Vered Shwartz, Bar-Ilan University, Ramat Gan, Isreal
Kiril Simov, Bulgarian Academy of Sciences, Sofia, Bulgaria
Michael Spranger, Sony Computer Science Laboratories Inc., Tokyo, Japan
Armand Vilalta, Barcelona Supercomputing Center (BSC), Barcelona, Spain
Arkaitz Zubiaga, University of Warwick, Coventry, UK

Table of Contents

Conference Program

Replicated Siamese LSTM in Ticketing System for Similarity Learning and Retrieval in Asymmetric Texts
Pankaj Gupta, Bernt Andrassy and Hinrich Schütze

Word-Embedding based Content Features for Automated Oral Proficiency Scoring
Su-Youn Yoon, Anastassia Loukina, Chong Min Lee, Matthew Mulholland, Xinhao Wang and Ikkyu Choi

Automatically Linking Lexical Resources with Word Sense Embedding Models
Luis Nieto Piña and Richard Johansson

Transferred Embeddings for Igbo Similarity, Analogy, and Diacritic Restoration Tasks
Ignatius Ezeani, Ikechukwu Onyenwe and Mark Hepple

Towards Enhancing Lexical Resource and Using Sense-annotations of OntoSenseNet for Sentiment Analysis
Sreekavitha Parupalli, Vijjini Anvesh Rao and Radhika Mamidi

Knowledge Representation with Conceptual Spaces
Steven Schockaert

Knowledge Representation and Extraction at Scale
Christos Christodoulopoulos

Replicated Siamese LSTM in Ticketing System for Similarity Learning and Retrieval in Asymmetric Texts

Pankaj Gupta[1,2] **Bernt Andrassy**[1] **Hinrich Schütze**[2]
[1]Corporate Technology, Machine-Intelligence (MIC-DE), Siemens AG Munich, Germany
[2]CIS, University of Munich (LMU) Munich, Germany
pankaj.gupta@siemens.com | bernt.andrassy@siemens.com
pankaj.gupta@campus.lmu.de | inquiries@cis.lmu.de

Abstract

The goal of our industrial ticketing system is to retrieve a relevant solution for an input query, by matching with historical tickets stored in knowledge base. A query is comprised of subject and description, while a historical ticket consists of subject, description and solution. To retrieve a relevant solution, we use textual similarity paradigm to learn similarity in the query and historical tickets. The task is challenging due to significant term mismatch in the query and ticket pairs of asymmetric lengths, where subject is a short text but description and solution are multi-sentence texts. We present a novel Replicated Siamese LSTM model to learn similarity in asymmetric text pairs, that gives 22% and 7% gain (Accuracy@10) for retrieval task, respectively over unsupervised and supervised baselines. We also show that the topic and distributed semantic features for short and long texts improved both similarity learning and retrieval.

1 Introduction

Semantic Textual Similarity (STS) is the task to find out if the text pairs mean the same thing. The important tasks in Natural Language Processing (NLP), such as Information Retrieval (IR) and text understanding may be improved by modeling the underlying semantic similarity between texts.

With recent progress in deep learning, the STS task has gained success using LSTM (Mueller and Thyagarajan, 2016) and CNN (Yin et al., 2016) based architectures; however, these approaches model the underlying semantic similarity between example pairs, each with a single sentence or phrase with term overlaps. In the domain of question retrieval (Cai et al., 2011; Zhang et al., 2014), users retrieve historical questions which precisely match their questions (single sentence) semantically equivalent or relevant. However, we investigate similarity learning between texts of asymmetric lengths, such as short (phrase) Vs longer (paragraph/documents) with significant term mismatch. The application of textual understanding in retrieval becomes more challenging when the relevant document-sized retrievals are stylistically distinct with the input short texts. Learning a similarity metric has gained much research interest, however due to limited availability of labeled data and complex structures in variable length sentences, the STS task becomes a hard problem. The performance of IR system is sub-optimal due to significant term mismatch in similar texts (Zhao, 2012), limited annotated data and complex structures in variable length sentences. We address the challenges in a real-world industrial application.

Our ticketing system (Figure 1(a)) consists of a query and historical tickets (Table 1). A query (reporting issue, q) has 2 components: *subject* (SUB) and *description* (DESC), while a historical ticket (t) stored in the knowledge base (KB) has 3 components: SUB, DESC and *solution* (SOL). A SUB is a short text, but DESC and SOL consist of multiple sentences. Table 1 shows that SUB $\in q$ and SUB $\in$ t are semantically similar and few terms in SUB $\in q$ overlap with DESC $\in$ t. However, the expected SOL $\in$ t is distinct from both SUB and DESC $\in q$. The goal is to retrieve an optimal action (i.e. SOL from t) for the input q.

To improve retrieval for an input q, we adapt the Siamese LSTM (Mueller and Thyagarajan, 2016) for similarity learning in asymmetric text pairs, using the available information in q and t. For instance,

Proceedings of SemDeep-3, the 3rd Workshop on Semantic Deep Learning, pages 1–11
Santa Fe, New Mexico, USA, August 20, 2018.

QUERY (q)

SUB: GT Trip - Low Frequency Pulsations

DESC: GT Tripped due to a sudden increase in Low Frequency Pulsations. The machine has been restarted and is now operating normally. Alarm received was: GT XXX Low Frequency Pulsation.

HISTORICAL TICKET (t)

SUB: Narrow Frequency Pulsations

DESC: Low and Narrow frequency pulsations were detected. The peak value for the Low Frequency Pulsations is ## mbar.

SOL: XXXX combustion support is currently working on the issue. The action is that the machine should not run until resolved.

Table 1: Example of a Query and Historical Ticket

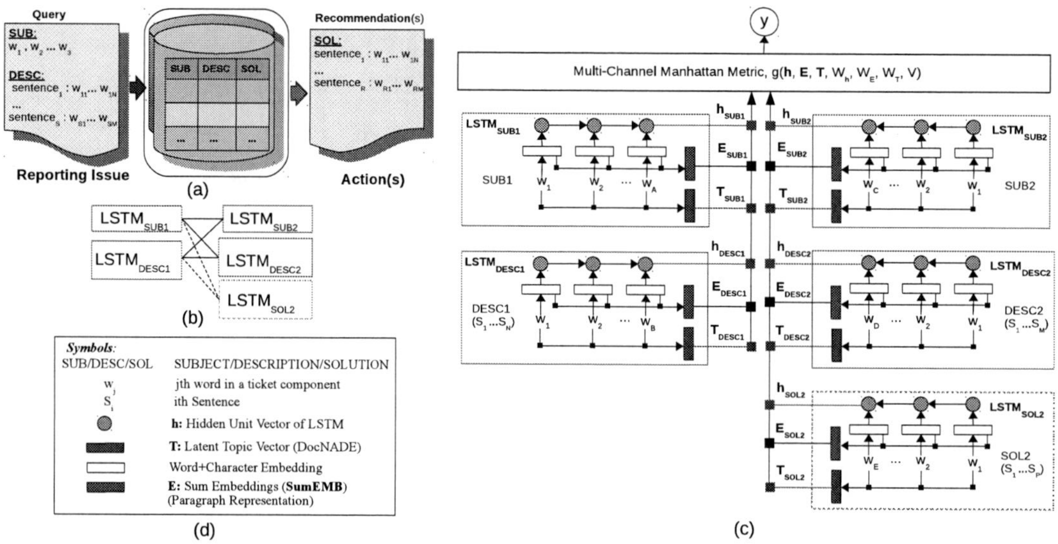

Figure 1: (a): Intelligent Ticketing System (ITS) (b): High-level illustration of Siamese LSTM for cross-level pairwise similarity. (c): Replicated Siamese with multi-channel (SumEMB, LSTM and topic vectors) and multi-level (SUB, DESC and/or SOL) inputs in the objective function, g. y: similarity score. The dotted lines indicate ITS output. (d): Symbols used.

we compute *multi-level* similarity between (SUB $\in q$, SUB $\in$ t) and (DESC $\in q$, DESC $\in$ t). However, observe in Table 1 that the *cross-level* similarities such as between (SUB $\in q$, DESC $\in$ t), (DESC $\in q$, SUB $\in$ t) or (SUB $\in q$, SOL $\in$ t), etc. can supplement IR performance. See Figure 1(b).

The *contributions* of this paper are as follows: (1) Propose a novel architecture (Replicated Siamese LSTM) for similarity learning in asymmetric texts via multi-and-cross-level semantics (2) Investigate distributed and neural topic semantics for similarity learning via multiple channels (3) Demonstrate a gain of 22% and 7% in Accuracy@10 for retrieval, respectively over unsupervised and supervised baselines in the industrial application of a ticketing system.

2 Methodology

Siamese networks (Chopra et al., 2005) are dual-branch networks with tied weights and an objective function. The aim of training is to learn text pair representations to form a highly structured space where they reflect complex semantic relationships. Figure 1 shows the proposed Replicated Siamese neural network architecture such that ($LSTM_{SUB1}$+$LSTM_{DESC1}$) = ($LSTM_{SUB2}$+$LSTM_{DESC2}$+$LSTM_{SOL2}$), to learn similarities in asymmetric texts, where a query (SUB1+DESC1) is stylistically distinct from a historical ticket (SUB2+DESC2+SOL2).

Note, the *query components are suffixed by "1" and historical ticket components by "2"* in context of the following work for pairwise comparisons.

$$g(h, E, T, W_h, W_E, W_T, V) =$$

$$\exp\Big(- \sum_{p \in \{SUB1, DESC1\}} \sum_{q \in \{SUB2, DESC2, SOL2\}} V_{\{p,q\}} \left(W_h \|h_p - h_q\|_1 + W_E \|E_p - E_q\|_1 + W_T \|T_p - T_q\|_1 \right)\Big) \quad (1)$$

Figure 2: Multi-Channel Manhattan Metric

2.1 Replicated, Multi-and-Cross-Level, Multi-Channel Siamese LSTM

Manhattan LSTM (Mueller and Thyagarajan, 2016) learns similarity in text pairs, each with a single sentence; however, we advance the similarity learning task in asymmetric texts pairs consisting of one or more sentences, where similarity is computed between different-sized subject and description or solution texts. As the backbone of our work, we compute similarity scores to learn a highly structured space via LSTM (Hochreiter and Schmidhuber, 1997) for representation of each pair of the query (SUB1 and DESC1) or historical ticket (SUB2, DESC2 and SOL2) components, which includes multi-level (SUB1-SUB2, DESC1-DESC2) and cross-level (SUB1-DESC2, SUB1-SOL2, etc.) asymmetric textual similarities, Figure 1(b) and (c). To accumulate the semantics of variable-length sentences ($x_1, ..., x_T$), recurrent neural networks (RNNs) (Vu et al., 2016a; Gupta et al., 2016; Gupta and Andrassy, 2018), especially the LSTMs (Hochreiter and Schmidhuber, 1997) have been successful.

LSTMs are superior in learning long range dependencies through their memory cells. Like the standard RNN (Mikolov et al., 2010; Gupta et al., 2015a; Vu et al., 2016b), LSTM sequentially updates a hidden-state representation, but it introduces a memory state c_t and three gates that control the flow of information through the time steps. An output gate o_t determines how much of c_t should be exposed to the next node. An input gate i_t controls how much the input x_t be stored in memory, while the forget gate f_t determines what should be forgotten from memory. The dynamics:

$$\begin{aligned}
i_t &= \sigma(W_i x_t + U_i h_{t-1}) \\
f_t &= \sigma(W_f x_t + U_f h_{t-1}) \\
o_t &= \sigma(W_o x_t + U_o h_{t-1}) \\
\tilde{c}_t &= tanh(W_c x_t + U_c h_{t-1}) \\
c_t &= i_t \odot \tilde{c}_t + f_t \odot c_{t-1} \\
h_t &= o_t \odot tanh(c_t)
\end{aligned} \quad (2)$$

where $\sigma(x) = \frac{1}{1+e^{-x}}$ and $\tanh(x) = \frac{e^x - e^{-x}}{e^x + e^{-x}}$. The proposed architecture, Figure 1(c) is composed of multiple uni-directional LSTMs each for subject, description and solution within the Siamese framework, where the weights at over levels are shared between the left and right branch of the network. Therefore, the name *replicated.*

Each LSTM learns a mapping from space of variable length sequences, including asymmetric texts, to a hidden-state vector, h. Each sentence ($w_1, ...w_T$) is passed to LSTM, which updates hidden state via eq 2. A final encoded representation (e.g. h_{SUB1}, h_{SUB2} in Figure 1(c)) is obtained for each query or ticket component. A single LSTM is run over DESC and SOL components, consisting of one or more sentences. Therefore, the name *multi-level* Siamese.

The representations across the text components (SUB DESC or SOL) are learned in order to maximize the similarity and retrieval for a query with the historical tickets. Therefore, the name *cross-level* Siamese.

The sum-average strategy over word embedding (Mikolov et al., 2010) for short and longer texts has demonstrated a strong baseline for text classification (Joulin et al., 2016) and pairwise similarity learning (Wieting et al., 2016). This simple baseline to represent sentences as bag of words (BoW) inspires us to use the BoW for each query or historical ticket component, for instance E_{SUB1}. We refer the approach as *SumEMB* in the context of this paper.

We supplement the similarity metric (g) with *SumEMB* (E), latent topic (T) (section 2.2) and hidden vectors (h) of LSTM for each text component from both the Siamese branches. Therefore, the name *multi-channel* Siamese.

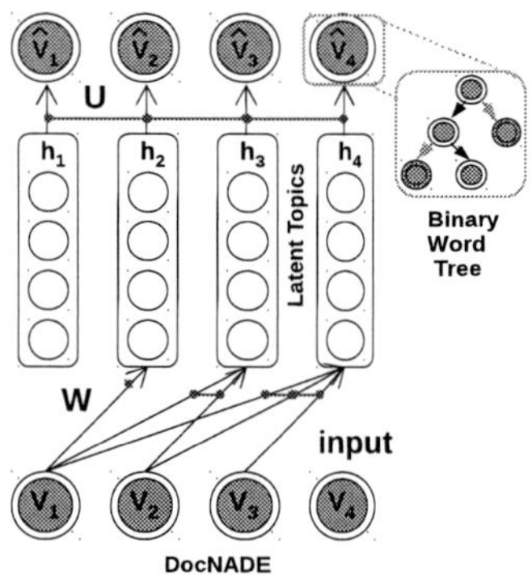

Figure 3: DocNADE: Neural Autoregressive Topic Model

Parameter	*Search*	*Optimal*
E	[350]	350
T	[20, 50, 100]	100
h	[50, 100]	50
W_h	[0.6, 0.7, 0.8]	0.7
W_E	[0.3, 0.2, 0.1]	0.1
W_T	[0.3, 0.2, 0.1]	0.2
$V_{SUB1-SUB2}$	[0.3, 0.4	0.3
$V_{DESC1-DESC2}$	[0.3, 0.4]	0.3
$V_{SUB1-DESC2}$	[0.10, 0.15, 0.20]	0.20
$V_{SUB1-SOL2}$	[0.10, 0.15, 0.20]	0.10
$V_{DESC1-SOL2}$	[0.10, 0.15, 0.20]	0.10

Table 2: Hyperparameters in the Replicated Siamese LSTM (experiment #No:22)

2.2 Neural Auto-Regressive Topic Model

Topic models such as Latent Dirichlet allocation (LDA) (Blei et al., 2003) and Replicated Softmax (RSM) (Hinton and Salakhutdinov, 2009; Gupta et al., 2018c) have been popular in learning meaningful representations of unlabeled text documents. Recently, a new type of topic model called the Document Neural Autoregressive Distribution Estimator (DocNADE) (Larochelle and Lauly, 2012; Zheng et al., 2016; Gupta et al., 2018a) was proposed and demonstrated the state-of- the-art performance for text document modeling. DocNADE models are advanced variants of Restricted Boltzmann Machine (Hinton, 2002; Salakhutdinov et al., 2007; Gupta et al., 2015b; Gupta et al., 2015c), and have shown to outperform LDA and RSM in terms of both log-likelihood of the data and document retrieval. In addition, the training complexity of a DocNADE model scales logarithmically with vocabulary size, instead linear as in RSM. The features are important for an industrial task along with quality performance. Therefore, we adopt DocNADE model for learning latent representations of tickets and retrieval in unsupervised fashion. See Larochelle and Lauly (2012) and Gupta et al. (2018a) for further details, and Figure 3 for the DocNADE architecture, where we extract the last hidden topic layer (h_4) to compute document representation.

2.3 Multi-Channel Manhattan Metric

Chopra et al. (2005) indicated that using l_2 instead of l_1 norm in similarity metric can lead to undesirable plateaus. Mueller and Thyagarajan (2016) showed stable and improved results using Manhattan distance over cosine similarity.

Mueller and Thyagarajan (2016) used a Manhattan metric (l_1-norm) for similarity learning in single sentence pairs. However, we adapt the similarity metric for 2-tuple (SUB1, DESC1) vs 3-tuple (SUB2, DESC2 and SOL2) pairs, where the error signals are back-propagated in the multiple levels and channels during training to force the Siamese network to entirely capture the semantic differences across the query and historical tickets components. The similarity metric, $g \in [0,1]$ is given in eq 1, where $||\cdot||$ is l_1 norm. W_h, W_E and W_T are the three channels weights for h, E and and T, respectively. The weights (V) are the multi-level weights between the ticket component pairs. Observe that a single weight is being used in the ordered ticket component pairs, for instance $V_{SUB1-DESC2}$ is same as $V_{DESC2-SUB1}$.

3 Evaluation and Analysis

We evaluate the proposed method on our industrial data for textual similarity learning and retrieval tasks in the ticketing system. Table 4 shows the different model configurations used in the following exper-

Held-out	*Perplexity* (100 topics)			
Ticket	$M1$: SUB+DESC		$M2$: SUB+DESC+SOL	
Component	LDA	DocNADE	LDA	DocNADE
DESC	380	**362**	565	**351**
SUB+DESC	480	**308**	515	**289**
SUB+DESC+SOL	553	**404**	541	**322**

(a)

Query	Perplexity (100 topics)			
Component	DocNADE:M1		DocNADE:M2	
	$\|Q\|_L$	$\|Q\|_U$	$\|Q\|_L$	$\|Q\|_U$
DESC1	192	177	132	118
SUB1+DESC1	164	140	130	118

(b)

Table 3: **(a)** Perplexity by DocNADE and LDA trained with $M1$: SUB+DESC or $M2$: SUB+DESC+SOL on all tickets and evaluated on 50 held-out tickets with their respective components or their combination. Observe that when DocNADE is trained with SUB+DESC+SOL, it performs better when training with SUB+DESC+SOL and outperforms LDA. **(b)** Perplexity by DocNADE: $M1$ trained on SUB+ DESC and $M2$ on SUB+DESC+SOL of the historical tickets.

Model	**Model Configuration**
$T\,(X1–X2)$	Compute Similarity using topic vector (T) pairs of a query ($X1$) and historical ticket ($X2$) components
$E\,(X1–X2)$	Compute Similarity using embedding vector (E) pairs of a query ($X1$) and historical ticket ($X2$) components
$X + Y + Z$	Merge text components (SUB, DESC or SOL), representing a single document
$T\,(X1 + Y1–X2 + Y2 + Z2)$	Compute Similarity using topic vector (T) pairs of a query ($X1 + Y1$) and historical ticket ($X2 + Y2 + Z2$) components
S-LSTM ($X1–X2$)	Compute Similarity using Standard Siamese LSTM on a query ($X1$) and historical ticket ($X2$) components
ML ($X1–X2$, $Y1–Y2$)	Multi-level Replicated Siamese LSTM. Compute similarity in ($X1–X2$) and ($Y1–Y2$) components of a query and historical ticket
CL (X, Y, Z)	Cross-level Replicated Siamese LSTM. Compute similarity in ($X1–Y2$), ($X1–Z2$), ($Y1–X2$) and ($Y1–Z2$) pairs

Table 4: Different model configurations for the experimental setups and evaluations. See Figure 1(c) for LSTM configurations.

imental setups. We use Pearson correlation, Spearman correlation and Mean Squared Error[1] (MSE) metrics for STS and 9 different metrics (Table 5) for IR task.

3.1 Industrial Dataset for Ticketing System

Our industrial dataset consist of queries and historical tickets. As shown in Table 1, a query consists of *subject* and *description* texts, while a historical ticket in knowledge base (KB) consists of *subject*, *description* and *solution* texts. The goal of the ITS is to automatically recommend an optimal action i.e. *solution* for an input query, retrieved from the existing KB.

There are $\mathfrak{T} = 949$ historical tickets in the KB, out of which 421 pairs are labeled with their relatedness score. We randomly split the labeled pairs by 80-20% for train (P_{tr}) and development (P_{dev}). The relatedness labels are: *YES* (similar that provides correct solution), *REL* (does not provide correct solution, but close to a solution) and *NO* (not related, not relevant and provides no correct solution). We convert the labels into numerical scores [1,5], where *YES*:5.0, *REL*:3.0 and *NO*:1.0. The average length (#words) of SUB, DESC and SOL are 4.6, 65.0 and 74.2, respectively.

The end-user (customer) additionally supplies 28 unique queries (Q_U) (exclusive to the historical tickets) to test system capabilities to retrieve the optimal solution(s) by computing 28×949 pairwise ticket similarities. We use these queries for the end-user qualitative evaluation for the 28×10 proposals (top 10 retrievals for each query).

3.2 Experimental Setup: Unsupervised

We establish baseline for similarity and retrieval by the following two unsupervised approaches:

(1) Topic Semantics T: As discussed in section 2.2, we use DocNADE topic model to learn document representation. To train, we take 50 held-out samples from the historical tickets $\mathfrak{T}$. We compute perplexity on 100 topics for each ticket component from the held-out set, comparing LDA and DocNADE models trained individually with SUB+DESC ($M1$) and SUB+DESC+SOL texts[2] ($M2$). Table 3a shows that DocNADE outperforms LDA.

[1] http://alt.qcri.org/semeval2016/task1/

[2] +: merge texts to treat them as a single document

#No	Model (Query-Historical Ticket)	Similarity Task			Retrieval Task								
		r	ρ	MSE	MAP@1	MAP@5	MAP@10	MRR@1	MRR@5	MRR@10	Acc@1	Acc@5	Acc@10
1	T (SUB1–SUB2) (**unsupervised baseline**)	0.388	0.330	5.122	0.08	0.08	0.07	1.00	0.28	0.10	0.04	0.19	0.30
2	T (SUB1–DESC2)	0.347	0.312	3.882	0.09	0.07	0.07	0.00	0.05	0.08	0.04	0.13	0.21
3	T (DESC1–SUB2)	0.321	0.287	3.763	0.08	0.09	0.09	0.00	0.05	0.11	0.03	0.20	0.31
4	T (DESC1–DESC2)	0.402	0.350	3.596	0.08	0.08	0.08	0.00	0.04	0.10	0.03	0.19	0.33
5	T (SUB1–SUB2+DESC2)	0.413	0.372	3.555	0.09	0.09	0.08	0.00	0.05	0.11	0.04	0.20	0.32
6	T (SUB1+DESC1–SUB2)	0.330	0.267	3.630	0.09	0.10	0.09	0.00	0.26	0.12	0.04	0.23	0.35
7	T (SUB1+DESC1–DESC2)	0.400	0.350	3.560	0.07	0.08	0.08	0.00	0.00	0.10	0.03	0.19	0.35
8	T (SUB1+DESC1–SUB2+DESC2)	0.417	0.378	3.530	0.05	0.07	0.08	0.00	0.07	0.11	0.03	0.22	0.37
9	T (SUB1+DESC1–SUB2+DESC2+SOL2)	0.411	0.387	3.502	0.09	0.09	0.08	0.00	0.06	0.12	0.04	0.20	0.40
11	E (SUB1–SUB2) (**unsupervised baseline**)	0.141	0.108	3.636	0.39	0.38	0.36	0.00	0.03	0.08	0.02	0.13	0.24
12	E (DESC1–DESC2)	0.034	0.059	4.201	**0.40**	**0.40**	**0.39**	0.00	0.10	0.07	0.03	0.12	0.18
13	E (SUB1+DESC1–SUB2+DESC2)	0.103	0.051	5.210	0.16	0.16	0.15	0.00	0.03	0.11	0.07	0.16	0.20
14	E (SUB1+DESC1–SUB2+DESC2+SOL2)	0.063	0.041	5.607	0.20	0.17	0.16	0.00	0.03	0.13	0.05	0.13	0.22
15	S-LSTM(SUB1–SUB2) (**supervised baseline**)	0.530	0.501	3.778	0.272	0.234	0.212	0.000	0.128	0.080	0.022	0.111	0.311
16	S-LSTM (DESC1–DESC2)	0.641	0.586	3.220	0.277	0.244	0.222	0.100	**0.287**	0.209	0.111	0.3111	0.489
17	S-LSTM (SUB1+DESC1–SUB2+DESC2)	0.662	0.621	2.992	0.288	0.251	0.232	0.137	0.129	0.208	0.111	0.342	0.511
18	S-LSTM (SUB1+DESC1–SUB2+DESC2+SOL2)	0.693	0.631	2.908	0.298	0.236	0.241	0.143	0.189	0.228	0.133	0.353	0.548
19	ML-LSTM (SUB1–SUB2, DESC1–DESC2)	0.688	0.644	2.870	0.290	0.255	0.234	0.250	0.121	0.167	0.067	0.289	0.533
20	+ CL-LSTM (SUB, DESC, SOL)	0.744	0.680	2.470	0.293	0.259	0.238	0.143	0.179	0.286	**0.178**	0.378	0.564
21	+ weighted channels (h*0.8, E*0.2)	0.758	0.701	2.354	0.392	0.376	0.346	**0.253**	0.176	0.248	0.111	0.439	0.579
22	+ weighted channels (h*0.7, E*0.1, T*0.2)	**0.792**	**0.762**	**2.052**	0.382	0.356	0.344	0.242	0.202	**0.288**	0.133	**0.493**	**0.618**

Table 5: Results on Development set: Pearson correlation (r), Spearmans rank correlation coefficient (ρ), Mean Squared Error (MSE), Mean Average Precision@k (MAP@k), Mean Reciprocal Rank@k (MRR@k) and Accuracy@k (Acc@k) for the multi-level (ML) and cross-level (CL) similarity learning, and retrieving the k-most similar tickets for each query (SUB1+DESC1). **#[1-14]**: Unsupervised baselines with DocNADE (T) and SumEMB (E). **#[15-18]**: Supervised Standard Siamese baselines. **#[19-22]**: Supervised Replicated Siamese with multi-channel and cross-level features.

Model	Similarity Task			Retrieval Task								
	r	ρ	MSE	MAP@1	MAP@5	MAP@10	MRR@1	MRR@5	MRR@10	Acc@1	Acc@5	Acc@10
T (SUB1-SUB2)	0.414	0.363	5.062	0.04	0.03	0.03	**0.29**	0.24	0.10	0.01	0.17	0.28
T (SUB1-DESC2)	0.399	0.362	3.791	0.04	0.03	0.03	0.00	0.05	0.07	0.03	0.12	0.19
T (DESC1-SUB2)	0.371	0.341	3.964	0.05	0.06	0.05	0.25	0.07	0.11	0.04	0.21	0.33
T (DESC1-DESC2)	0.446	0.398	3.514	0.05	0.05	0.04	0.00	0.04	0.10	0.04	0.18	0.34
T (SUB1-SUB2+DESC2)	0.410	0.370	3.633	0.05	0.04	0.04	0.00	0.12	0.08	0.04	0.13	0.20
T (SUB1+DESC2-SUB2)	0.388	0.326	3.561	0.06	0.06	0.05	0.25	**0.29**	0.13	0.05	0.22	0.38
T (SUB1+DESC1-DESC2)	0.443	0.396	3.477	0.04	0.04	0.04	0.00	0.00	0.10	0.03	0.17	0.37
T (SUB1+DESC1, SUB2+DESC2)	**0.466**	**0.417**	3.460	0.05	0.05	0.04	0.00	0.06	0.11	0.03	**0.24**	0.37
T (SUB1+DESC1, SUB2+DESC2+SOL2)	0.418	0.358	**3.411**	**0.07**	0.06	**0.06**	0.00	0.09	**0.14**	0.05	0.20	**0.39**

Table 6: DocNADE ($M2$) performance for the queries $Q_L \in (P_{tr} + P_{dev})$ in the labeled pairs in unsupervised fashion.

Next, we need to determine which DocNADE model ($M1$ or $M2$) is less perplexed to the queries. Therefore, we use $M1$ and $M2$ to evaluate DESC1 and SUB1+DESC1 components of the two sets of queries: (1) Q_L is the set of queries from labeled (421) pairs and (2) Q_U is the end-user set. Table 3b shows that $M2$ performs better than $M1$ for both the sets of queries with DESC1 or SUB1+DESC1 texts. We choose $M2$ version of the DocNADE to setup baseline for the similarity learning and retrieval in unsupervised fashion.

To compute a similarity score for the given query q and historical ticket t where (q, t)$\in P_{dev}$, we first compute a latent topic vector (T) each for q and t using DocNADE ($M2$) and then apply the similarity metric g (eq 1). To evaluate retrieval for q, we retrieve the top 10 similar tickets, ranked by the similarity scores on their topic vectors. Table 5 (#No [1-9]) shows the performance of DocNADE for similarity and retrieval tasks. Observe that #9 achieves the best MSE (3.502) and Acc@10 (0.40) out of [1-9], suggesting that the topic vectors of query (SUB1+DESC1) and historical ticket (SUB2+DESC2+SOL2) are the key in recommending a relevant SOL2. See the performance of DocNADE for all labeled pairs i.e. queries and historical tickets ($P_{tr} + P_{dev}$) in the Table 6.

(2) Distributional Semantics E: Beyond topic models, we establish baseline using the SumEMB method (section 2.1), where an embedding vector E is computed following the topic semantics approach. The experiments #11-14 show that the SumEMB results in lower performance for both the tasks, suggesting a need of a supervised paradigm in order to learn similarities in asymmetric texts. Also, the comparison with DocNADE indicates that the topic features are important in the retrieval of tickets.

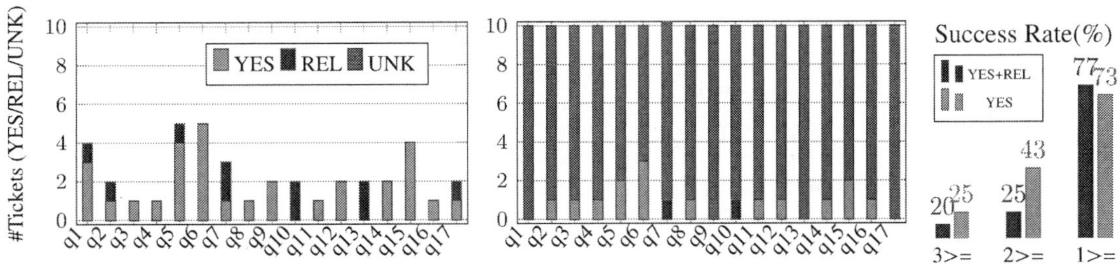

Figure 4: Evaluation on End-user Queries (sub-sample). UNK: Unknown. (Left) Gold Data: The count of similar (YES) and relevant (REL) tickets for each query (q1-q17). (Middle) ITS Results: For each query, ITS proposes the top 10 YES/REL retrievals. The plot depicts the count of YES/REL proposals matched out of the top 10 gold proposals for each q. UNK may include YES, REL or NO, not annotated in the gold pairs. (Right) Success Rate: YES: percentage of correct similar(YES) proposal out of the top 10; YES+REL: percentage of correct similar (YES) and relevant(REL) proposals out of the top 10.

3.3 Experimental Setup: Supervised

For semantic relatedness scoring, we train the Replicated Siamese, using backpropagation-through-time under the Mean Squared Error (MSE) loss function (after rescaling the training-set relatedness labels to lie $\in [0, 1]$). After training, we apply an additional non-parametric regression step to obtain better-calibrated predictions $\in [1, 5]$, same as (Mueller and Thyagarajan, 2016). We then evaluate the trained model for IR task, where we retrieve the top 10 similar results (SUB2+DESC2+SOL2), ranked by their similarity scores, for each query (SUB1+DESC1) in the development set and compute MAP@K, MRR@K and Acc@K, where K=1, 5, and 10.

We use 300-dimensional pre-trained *word2vec*[3] embeddings for input words, however, to generalize beyond the limited vocabulary in *word2vec* due to industrial domain data with technical vocabulary, we also employ char-BLSTM (Lample et al., 2016) to generate additional embeddings (=50 dimension[4]).The resulting dimension for word embeddings is 350. We use 50-dimensional hidden vector, h_t, memory cells, c_t and Adadelta (Zeiler, 2012) with dropout and gradient clipping (Pascanu et al., 2013) for optimization. The topics vector (T) size is 100. We use python NLTK toolkit[5] for sentence tokenization. See Table 2 for the hyperparameters in Replicated Siamese LSTM for experiment #No:22.

3.4 Results: State-of-the-art Comparisons

Table 5 shows the similarity and retrieval scores for unsupervised and supervised baseline methods. The #9, #18 and #20 show that the supervised approach performs better than unsupervised topic models. #17 and #19 suggest that the multi-level Siamese improves (Acc@10: 0.51 vs. 0.53) both STS and IR. Comparing #18 and #20, the cross-level Siamese shows performance gains (Acc@10: 0.55 vs. 0.57). Finally, #21 and #22 demonstrates improved similarity (MSE: 2.354 vs. 2.052) and retrieval (Acc@10: 0.58 vs. 0.62) due to weighted multi-channel (h, E and T) inputs.

The replicated Siamese (#22) with different features best results in 2.052 for MSE and 0.618 (= 61.8%) for Acc@10. We see 22% and 7% gain in Acc@10 for retrieval task, respectively over unsupervised (#9 vs. #22: 0.40 vs. 0.62) and supervised (#18 vs. #22: 0.55 vs. 0.62) baselines. The experimental results suggest that the similarity learning in supervised fashion improves the ranking of relevant tickets.

3.5 Success Rate: End-User Evaluation

We use the trained similarity model to retrieve the top 10 similar tickets from KB for each end-user query Q_U, and compute the number of correct similar and relevant tickets. For ticket ID $q6$ (Figure 4, Middle),

[3]Publicly available at: code.google.com/p/word2vec

[4]Run forward-backward character LSTM for every word and concatenate the last hidden units (25 dimension each)

[5]http://www.nltk.org/api/nltk.tokenize.html

Query	Recommendation_1	Recommendation_2	Recommendation_3
SUB: GT Trip - Low Frequency Pulsations **DESC:** GT Tripped due to a sudden increase in Low Frequency Pulsations. The machine has been restarted and is now operating normally. Alarm received was: GT XXX Low Frequency Pulsation	**SUB:** Narrow Frequency Pulsations **DESC:** Low and Narrow frequency pulsations were detected. The peak value for the Low Frequency Pulsations is ## mbar. **SOL:** XXXXX combustion support is currently working on the issue. The recommended action for now is that the machine XXXX at **load** XXXX ## **MW**.	**SUB:** Low frequency pulsations **DESC:** High level low frequency pulsations were detected when active **load** is XXXX. **SOL:** Since the machine is running with XXXX, the XXX be changed in the register. After adjustment is complete, monitor the machine behavior between ## **MW** to ## **load**.	**SUB:** GT3 - High Low Frequency Pulsation alarms after trip **DESC:** Yesterday, after Steam Turbine tripped, GT-3 experienced high Low Frequency Pulsation alarm. The**load** of GT-3 was ## **MW** and went up as high as ## **MW**. During the time, Low Frequency Pulsation for 3 pulsation devices went up as high as ##. The Low frequency pulsation was a XXX. **SOL:** A **load** XXXX from ## **MW** to ## **MW** is an event XXX the unit XXXX trip. The XXXX to low frequency pulsation during similar event, should be XXXX. Check that XXXX from after the XXXX (XX005/XX01) into combustion chamber (XX030/XX01), XXXX should be XXXX. Repeat until XXXX is within the range of ## -##.
(Rank, Similarity Score)	(1, 4.75)	(2, 4.71)	(3, 4.60)
#Topics {**#83**, #7, #30}	{**#83**, #16, #30}	{#7, **#83**, #19}	{#7, **#83**, #19}

Table 7: Top-3 Tickets Retrieved and ordered by their (rank, similarity score) for an input test query. *#Topics*: the top 3 most probable associated topics. **SOL** of the retrieved tickets is returned as recommended action. Underline: Overlapping words; XXXX and ##: Confidential text and numerical terms.

3 out of 10 proposed tickets are marked similar, where the end-user expects 4 similar tickets (Figure 4, Left). For ticket ID $q1$, $q13$ and $q17$, the top 10 results do not include the corresponding expected tickets due to no term matches and we find that the similarity scores for all the top 10 tickets are close to 4.0 or higher, which indicates that the system proposes more similar tickets (than the expected tickets), not included in the gold annotations. The top 10 proposals are evaluated for each query by success rate (success, if N/10 proposals supply the expected solution). We compute success rate (Figure 4, Right) for (1 or more), (2 or more) and (3 or more) correct results out of the top 10 proposals.

4 Qualitative Inspections for STS and IR

Table 7 shows a real example for an input query, where the top 3 recommendations are proposed from the historical tickets using the trained Replicated Siamese model. The recommendations are ranked by their similarity scores with the query. The underline shows the overlapping texts.

We also show the most probable topics (#) that the query or each recommendation is associated with. The topics shown (Table 8) are learned from DocNADE model and are used in multi-channel network. Observe that the improved retrieval scores (Table 5 #22) are attributed to the overlapping topic semantics in query and the top retrievals. For instance, the topic #83 is the most probable topic feature for the query and recommendations. We found terms, especially *load* and *MW* in SOL (frequently appeared for other *Frequency Pulsations* tickets) that are captured in topics #7 and #83, respectively.

5 Related Work

Semantic Textual Similarity has diverse applications in information retrieval (Larochelle and Lauly, 2012; Gupta et al., 2018a), search, summarization (Gupta et al., 2011), recommendation systems, etc. For shared STS task in SemEval 2014, numerous researchers applied competitive methods that utilized both heterogeneous features (e.g. word overlap/similarity, negation modeling, sentence/phrase composition) as well as external resources (e.g. Wordnet (Miller, 1995)), along with machine learning approaches such as LSA (Zhao et al., 2014) and word2vec neural language model (Mikolov et al., 2013). In the domain of question retrieval (Cai et al., 2011; Zhang et al., 2014), users retrieve historical questions which precisely match their questions (single sentence) semantically equivalent or relevant.

Neural network based architectures, especially CNN (Yin et al., 2016), LSTM (Mueller and Thyagarajan, 2016), RNN encoder-decoder (Kiros et al., 2015), etc. have shown success in similarity learning

ID	Topic Words (Top 10)
#83	pulsation, frequency, low, load, high, pulsations, increase, narrow, XXXX, mw
#7	trip, turbine, vibration, gas, alarm, gt, time, tripped, pressure, load
#30	start, flame, unit, turbine, combustion, steam, temperature, compressor, XXXX, detector
#16	oil, XXXX, XXXX, pressure, kpa, dp, level, high, mbar, alarm
#19	valve, XXXX, fuel, valves, gas, bypass, check, control, XXXX, XXXX

Table 8: Topics Identifier and words captured by DocNADE

task in Siamese framework (Mueller and Thyagarajan, 2016; Chopra et al., 2005). These models are adapted to similarity learning in sentence pairs using complex learners. Wieting et al. (2016) observed that word vector averaging and LSTM for similarity learning perform better in short and long text pairs, respectively. Our learning objective exploits the multi-channel representations of short and longer texts and compute cross-level similarities in different components of the query and tickets pairs. Instead of learning similarity in a single sentence pair, we propose a novel task and neural architecture for asymmetric textual similarities. To our knowledge, this is the first advancement of Siamese architecture towards multi-and-cross level similarity learning in asymmetric text pairs with an industrial application.

6 Conclusion and Discussion

We have demonstrated deep learning application in STS and IR tasks for an industrial ticketing system. The results indicate that the proposed LSTM is capable of modeling complex semantics by explicit guided representations and does not rely on hand-crafted linguistic features, therefore being generally applicable to any domain. We have showed improved similarity and retrieval via the proposed multi-and-cross-level Replicated Siamese architecture, leading to relevant recommendations especially in industrial use-case. As far we we know, this is the first advancement of Siamese architecture for similarity learning and retrieval in asymmetric text pairs with an industrial application.

We address the challenges in a real-world industrial application of ticketing system. Industrial assets like power plants, production lines, turbines, etc. need to be serviced well because an unplanned outage always leads to significant financial loss. It is an established process in industry to report issues (via query) i.e. symptoms which hint at an operational anomaly to the service provider. This reporting usually leads to textual descriptions of the issue in a ticketing system. The issue is then investigated by service experts who evaluate recommended actions or solutions to the reported issue. The recommended actions or solutions are usually attached to the reported issues and form a valuable knowledge base on how to resolve issues. Since industrial assets tend to be similar over the various installations and since they don't change quickly it is expected that the issues occurring over the various installations may be recurring. Therefore, if for a new issue similar old issues could be easily found this would enable service experts to speed up the evaluation of recommended actions or solutions to the reported issue. The chosen approach is to evaluate the pairwise semantic similarity of the issues describing texts.

We have compared unsupervised and supervised approach for both similarity learning and retrieval tasks, where the supervised approach leads the other. However, we foresee significant gains with the larger amount of similarity data as the amount of labeled similarity data grows and the continuous feedback is incorporated for optimization within the industrial domain, where quality results are desired. In future work, we would also like to investigate attention (Bahdanau et al., 2014) mechanism and dependency (Socher et al., 2012; Gupta et al., 2018b) structures in computing tickets' representation.

Acknowledgements

We thank our colleagues Mark Buckley, Stefan Langer, Subburam Rajaram and Ulli Waltinger, and anonymous reviewers for their review comments. This research was supported by Bundeswirtschaftsministerium (`bmwi.de`), grant 01MD15010A (Smart Data Web) at Siemens AG- CT Machine Intelligence, Munich Germany.

References

Dzmitry Bahdanau, Kyunghyun Cho, and Yoshua Bengio. 2014. Neural machine translation by jointly learning to align and translate. In *Proceedings of the International Conference on Learning Representation*, Alberta, Canada.

David M Blei, Andrew Y Ng, and Michael I Jordan. 2003. Latent dirichlet allocation. *Journal of machine Learning research*, 3(Jan):993–1022.

Li Cai, Guangyou Zhou, Kang Liu, and Jun Zhao. 2011. Learning the latent topics for question retrieval in community qa. In *Proceedings of 5th International Joint Conference on Natural Language Processing*, pages 273–281, Chiang Mai, Thailand. Association of Computational Linguistics.

Sumit Chopra, Raia Hadsell, and Yann LeCun. 2005. Learning a similarity metric discriminatively, with application to face verification. In *2005 IEEE Computer Society Conference on Computer Vision and Pattern Recognition (CVPR)*, volume 1, pages 539–546, San Diego, CA, USA. IEEE.

Pankaj Gupta and Bernt Andrassy. 2018. Device and method for natural language processing. US Patent 2018-0,157,643.

Pankaj Gupta, Vijay Shankar Pendluri, and Ishant Vats. 2011. Summarizing text by ranking text units according to shallow linguistic features. Seoul, South Korea. IEEE.

Pankaj Gupta, Thomas Runkler, Heike Adel, Bernt Andrassy, Hans-Georg Zimmermann, and Hinrich Schütze. 2015a. Deep learning methods for the extraction of relations in natural language text. Technical report, Technical University of Munich, Germany.

Pankaj Gupta, Thomas Runkler, and Bernt Andrassy. 2015b. Keyword learning for classifying requirements in tender documents. Technical report, Technical University of Munich, Germany.

Pankaj Gupta, Udhayaraj Sivalingam, Sebastian Pölsterl, and Nassir Navab. 2015c. Identifying patients with diabetes using discriminative restricted boltzmann machines. Technical report, Technical University of Munich, Germany.

Pankaj Gupta, Hinrich Schütze, and Bernt Andrassy. 2016. Table filling multi-task recurrent neural network for joint entity and relation extraction. In *Proceedings of COLING 2016, the 26th International Conference on Computational Linguistics: Technical Papers*, pages 2537–2547, Osaka, Japan.

Pankaj Gupta, Florian Buettner, and Hinrich Schütze. 2018a. Document informed neural autoregressive topic models. Researchgate preprint doi: 10.13140/RG.2.2.12322.73925.

Pankaj Gupta, Subburam Rajaram, Bernt Andrassy, Thomas Runkler, and Hinrich Schütze. 2018b. Neural relation extraction within and across sentence boundaries. Researchgate preprint doi: 10.13140/RG.2.2.16517.04327.

Pankaj Gupta, Subburam Rajaram, Hinrich Schütze, and Bernt Andrassy. 2018c. Deep temporal-recurrent-replicated-softmax for topical trends over time. In *Proceedings of the 2018 Conference of the North American Chapter of the Association for Computational Linguistics: Human Language Technologies, Volume 1 (Long Papers)*, volume 1, pages 1079–1089, New Orleans, USA. Association of Computational Linguistics.

Geoffrey E Hinton and Ruslan R Salakhutdinov. 2009. Replicated softmax: an undirected topic model. In *Advances in neural information processing systems*, pages 1607–1614, Vancouver, Canada.

Geoffrey E Hinton. 2002. Training products of experts by minimizing contrastive divergence. *Neural computation*, 14(8):1771–1800.

Sepp Hochreiter and Jürgen Schmidhuber. 1997. Long short-term memory. *Neural computation*, 9(8):1735–1780.

Armand Joulin, Edouard Grave, Piotr Bojanowski, and Tomas Mikolov. 2016. Bag of tricks for efficient text classification. *arXiv preprint arXiv:1607.01759*.

Ryan Kiros, Yukun Zhu, Ruslan R Salakhutdinov, Richard Zemel, Raquel Urtasun, Antonio Torralba, and Sanja Fidler. 2015. Skip-thought vectors. In *Advances in neural information processing systems*, pages 3294–3302, Montreal, Canada.

Guillaume Lample, Miguel Ballesteros, Sandeep Subramanian, Kazuya Kawakami, and Chris Dyer. 2016. Neural architectures for named entity recognition. In *Proceedings of the 2016 Conference of the North American Chapter of the Association for Computational Linguistics: Human Language Technologies*, pages 260–270. Association for Computational Linguistics.

Hugo Larochelle and Stanislas Lauly. 2012. A neural autoregressive topic model. In *Advances in Neural Information Processing Systems 25 (NIPS 2012)*, pages 1607–1614, Lake Tahoe, USA. Curran Associates, Inc.

Tomáš Mikolov, Martin Karafiát, Lukáš Burget, Jan Černocký, and Sanjeev Khudanpur. 2010. Recurrent neural network based language model. In *Eleventh Annual Conference of the International Speech Communication Association*, page 3.

Tomas Mikolov, Ilya Sutskever, Kai Chen, Greg S Corrado, and Jeff Dean. 2013. Distributed representations of words and phrases and their compositionality. In *Advances in neural information processing systems*, pages 3111–3119, Lake Tahoe, USA.

G.A. Miller. 1995. Wordnet: A lexical database for english. *Communications of the ACM*, 38(11):3941.

Jonas Mueller and Aditya Thyagarajan. 2016. Siamese recurrent architectures for learning sentence similarity. In *the thirtieth AAAI conference on Artificial Intelligence*, volume 16, pages 2786–2792, Phoenix, Arizona USA.

Razvan Pascanu, Tomas Mikolov, and Yoshua Bengio. 2013. On the difficulty of training recurrent neural networks. In *Proceedings of the International Conference on Machine Learning*, pages 1310–1318, Atlanta, USA.

Ruslan Salakhutdinov, Andriy Mnih, and Geoffrey Hinton. 2007. Restricted boltzmann machines for collaborative filtering. In *Proceedings of the 24th International Conference on Machine learning*, pages 791–798, Oregon, USA. Association for Computing Machinery.

Richard Socher, Brody Huval, Christopher D Manning, and Andrew Y Ng. 2012. Semantic compositionality through recursive matrix-vector spaces. In *Proceedings of the 2012 joint conference on empirical methods in natural language processing and computational natural language learning*, pages 1201–1211, Jeju Island, Korea. Association for Computational Linguistics.

Ngoc Thang Vu, Heike Adel, Pankaj Gupta, and Hinrich Schütze. 2016a. Combining recurrent and convolutional neural networks for relation classification. In *Proceedings of the North American Chapter of the Association for Computational Linguistics: Human Language Technologies*, pages 534–539, San Diego, California USA. Association for Computational Linguistics.

Ngoc Thang Vu, Pankaj Gupta, Heike Adel, and Hinrich Schütze. 2016b. Bi-directional recurrent neural network with ranking loss for spoken language understanding. In *Proceedings of the Acoustics, Speech and Signal Processing (ICASSP)*, pages 6060–6064, Shanghai, China. IEEE.

John Wieting, Mohit Bansal, Kevin Gimpel, and Karen Livescu. 2016. Towards universal paraphrastic sentence embeddings. In *Proceedings of the International Conference on Learning Representations*, San Juan, Puerto Rico.

Wenpeng Yin, Hinrich Schuetze, Bing Xiang, and Bowen Zhou. 2016. Abcnn: Attention-based convolutional neural network for modeling sentence pairs. *Transactions of the Association for Computational Linguistics*, 4:259–272.

Matthew D Zeiler. 2012. Adadelta: An adaptive learning rate method. *arXiv preprint arXiv:1212.5701*.

Kai Zhang, Wei Wu, Haocheng Wu, Zhoujun Li, and Ming Zhou. 2014. Question retrieval with high quality answers in community question answering. In *Proceedings of the 23rd ACM International Conference on Conference on Information and Knowledge Management*, pages 371–380, Shanghai, China. Association for Computing Machinery.

Jiang Zhao, Tiantian Zhu, and Man Lan. 2014. Ecnu: One stone two birds: Ensemble of heterogenous measures for semantic relatedness and textual entailment. In *Proceedings of the 8th International Workshop on Semantic Evaluation (SemEval 2014)*, pages 271–277, Dublin, Ireland.

Le Zhao. 2012. Modeling and solving term mismatch for full-text retireval. *ACM SIGIR*, pages 117–118.

Yin Zheng, Yu-Jin Zhang, and Hugo Larochelle. 2016. A deep and autoregressive approach for topic modeling of multimodal data. *IEEE transactions on pattern analysis and machine intelligence*, 38(6):1056–1069.

Word-Embedding based Content Features for Automated Oral Proficiency Scoring

Su-Youn Yoon, Anastassia Loukina, Chong Min Lee,
Matthew Mulholland, Xinhao Wang and Ikkyu Choi
Educational Testing Service
660 Rosedale Road, Princeton, NJ, USA
syoon,aloukina,clee001,xwang002,mmulholland,ichoi001@ets.org

Abstract

In this study, we develop content features for an automated scoring system of non-native English speakers' spontaneous speech. The features calculate the lexical similarity between the question text and the ASR word hypothesis of the spoken response, based on traditional word vector models or word embeddings. The proposed features do not require any sample training responses for each question, and this is a strong advantage since collecting question-specific data is an expensive task, and sometimes even impossible due to concerns about question exposure. We explore the impact of these new features on the automated scoring of two different question types: (a) providing opinions on familiar topics and (b) answering a question about a stimulus material. The proposed features showed statistically significant correlations with the oral proficiency scores, and the combination of new features with the speech-driven features achieved a small but significant further improvement for the latter question type. Further analyses suggested that the new features were effective in assigning more accurate scores for responses with serious content issues.

1 Introduction

This study aims to develop new features to score the content of non-native speakers' spontaneous speech as a part of an automated oral proficiency scoring system. The system provides holistic proficiency scores using audio files and their transcriptions generated by an automated speech recognition (ASR) system. Previously, studies in automated speech scoring have mainly focused on assessment of fluency (Cucchiarini et al., 2000; Zechner et al., 2009), pronunciation (Witt and Young, 1997), and intonation and rhythm (Lai et al., 2013; Wang et al., 2015). More recently, researchers started exploring assessment of grammar (Chen and Zechner, 2011; Bhat and Yoon, 2015) and vocabulary(Yoon et al., 2012).

To date, limited studies have explored approaches to evaluating the content of spoken responses. Xie et al. (2012) explored content features based on the lexical similarity between the response and a set of sample responses for each question. A content-scoring component based on word vectors was also part of the automated scoring engine described by Cheng et al. (2014). In both of these studies, content features were developed to supplement other features measuring various aspects of speaking proficiency. Neither study reported the relative contributions of content and speech features to the system performance. Loukina et al. (2017) considered a content-scoring engine based on many sparse features such as unigrams and bigrams and trained on a large corpus of existing responses. They showed that this approach achieved performance comparable to that based on fluency and pronunciation, but there was only little improvement from combining the two sets of features.

Approaches like those above require a sizable amount of response data for each question, and collecting question-specific data is an expensive and difficult task. Furthermore, for high-stakes assessment this can be impossible due to concerns about question exposure. A content feature that does not require any test takers' responses for new questions has a strong advantage when scoring a large scale operational assessment.

Proceedings of SemDeep-3, the 3rd Workshop on Semantic Deep Learning, pages 12–22
Santa Fe, New Mexico, USA, August 20, 2018.

To address this issue, Higgins et al. (2006) developed a system for scoring off-topic essays without the need for question-specific responses; the system was based on similarity features between the question text and the test response. The performance of this system was lower than the benchmark system trained on question-specific responses, but it achieved a substantial improvement over a majority-based baseline. Louis and Higgins (2010) further improved this system by expanding question texts to include synonyms, inflected forms, and distributionally similar words to the question content. The performance of Louis and Higgins (2010) showed a substantial improvement for questions consisting of only a small amount of text. More recently, Evanini et al. (2013) developed a set of content features based on both the questions and listening and reading materials for automated speech scoring and reported significant correlations between these content features and the proficiency scores.

Various approaches based on deep-neural networks (DNN) and word-embeddings trained on large corpora have showed promising performance in various NLP tasks, such as document similarity detection (Kusner et al., 2015; Mueller and Thyagarajan, 2016; Neculoiu et al., 2016). In contrast to traditional similarity features, which are limited to a reliance on exact word matching, these new approaches have the advantage of capturing topically relevant words that are not identical. Yoon et al. (2017) and Rei and Cummins (2016) applied this approach to the task of off-topic detection in spoken responses and essays, respectively, and achieved substantial improvements over systems that only use word-matching.

In this study, we combine the approach suggested by Evanini et al. (2013) and with more recent advances in word embeddings and develop a new set of low-resource content features: these features are trained using the prompt text expanded with word-embeddings without relying on any pre-existing responses to a given question. We conducted the following research:

- Using the prompt texts included in each question, we developed two sets of content features: features based on the traditional content vector analysis (CVA) approach and features based on word embeddings.
- We trained automated scoring models using traditional speech-driven features and new content features and compared the performance of the models.
- We investigated the impact of question types on the performance of the content features and the automated scoring models. We provided an in-depth discussion about what aspects of the content can be assessed by these new content features.

2 Data

We used a large collection of spoken responses from an assessment of English proficiency for academic purposes[1]. The speaking section of the assessment was composed of 6 questions in which speakers were prompted to provide responses lasting between 45 and 60 seconds per question, resulting in approximately 5.5 minutes of speech per speaker. All questions extracted spontaneous speech.

Among the 6 questions, two questions (hereafter, Independent questions) asked examinees to provide information or opinions on familiar topics based on their personal experience or background knowledge. These questions were short and typically consisted of just a few sentences. The questions were designed to elicit responses based on personal experience or views on specific topics. Thus, the responses differed widely in their content. For the four remaining questions (hereafter, Integrated questions), test takers read and/or listened to stimulus materials and then answered a question relevant to the passage. We used 49 Independent questions and 98 Integrated questions in this study.

All responses were scored by trained raters using a 4-point scoring scale, where 1 indicates low speaking proficiency and 4 indicates high speaking proficiency. The rubrics consist of three major performance categories: delivery (pronunciation, intonation, rhythm, and fluency), language use (diversity, sophistication, and precision of vocabulary, and range, complexity, and accuracy of grammar), and topic development (progression of ideas, the degree of elaboration and completeness). We used the TOEFL iBT Speaking Test Rubrics, which provide descriptions about the typical characteristics of candidate

[1]The data is not publicly available.

performance for each score level. Approximately 10% of data set was double-scored, and an estimation of the inter-rater agreement was obtained from this dobule-scored sub-set. Both Pearson correlation and weighted kappa were 0.54 for Independent questions and 0.61 for Integrated questions.

We used 103, 868 and 49, 281 responses for training and evaluation of automated scoring models, respectively. In addition, 154, 992 responses were used to obtain an inverse-document frequency (*idf*) model for content features. The proposed features in this study did not use any question-specific sample responses for content model training, and thus, the *idf* Train set did not contain any responses answering the questions used in the scoring models. Finally, we used 73, 500 responses to train question-specific content models as a benchmark. The size of the data sets is summarized in Table 1.

Dataset	N. of questions	N. of responses			Responses per question
		Integrated	Independent	Total	
Scoring Model Train	147	34,426	69,442	103,868	706.6
Scoring Model Evaluation	147	16,298	32,983	49,281	335.2
idf Train	438	53,323	101,669	154,992	353.9
Question-specific Content Model Train	147 (same questions as Scoring Model partition)	73,500	24,500	49,000	500

Table 1: Number of questions, and responses for each partition

There were no overlaps among all datasets. There was a strong bias towards the middle scores (score 2 and 3); the most frequent score was 3 (50%) and followed by 2 (37%) with approximately 87% of the responses belonging to these two score levels. The percentages of responses with score 4 and score 1 were 9% and 4%, respectively.

3 Features

3.1 Content features

We developed two sets of content features using the prompt texts. The prompt texts consisted of the question sentences and optional listening and reading materials.

The first feature was a $tf - idf$ (term frequency - inverse document frequency) weighted cosine similarity score between the prompt text and the response (hereafter, *prompt-based CVA*). First, we obtained an *idf* model using the *idf* Train set which covered a wide range of questions except the 147 questions used in Scoring Model Train and Evaluation set. For each word in the *idf* Train set, we calculated the total number of responses divided by the number of responses containing it. Next, we built a question-specific *tf* model for each question. We converted the prompt text into a single vector and counted the number of the occurrences for each word.

The second set of features were features based on word-embeddings. Using the publicly available word embedding vectors trained on the Google News corpus by Mikolov et al. (2013), we developed the following two features used for the off-topic essay detection in Rei and Cummins (2016):

- averaged word embeddings: we created a vector for each question by mapping each word in the question text to a corresponding word embedding vector and averaging them. Next, we created a vector for a test response using the same process. Finally, we calculated the cosine similarity between the question vector and the response vector.
- *idf* weighted word embeddings: we calculated an *idf* weighted word embedding feature by scaling each word embedding vector by the corresponding *idf* weight and averaging the scaled vectors for the prompt and the response, separately. We calculated the cosine similarity between these two weighted vectors.

As a benchmark, we compare the proposed features, which are based only on the prompt materials, to a feature trained on the test takers' sample responses to the 147 questions (hereafter, *response-based CVA*). First, we obtained the ASR-based transcriptions for responses in the Question-specific Content Model Train set. All responses that answer the same question were converted into a single vector and a question-specific tf was built from this vector using the same process as the prompt-based tf model. Finally, we calculated a $tf - idf$ weighted cosine similarity score between a test response vector and the question-specific tf vector.

3.2 Speech-driven features

We used 35 features generated by an automated proficiency scoring system for non-native speakers' spontaneous speech. For a given spoken response, the system performs speech processing, including speech recognition, forced-alignment, pitch and power analysis, and generates a word hypotheses and time stamps. Given the word hypotheses and descriptive features of pitch/power, it generates the following five groups of features that capture information relevant to fluency and pronunciation. The numbers in parentheses are the number of features that belong to each group.

- Speech rate features (3): These features compute the words spoken per minute with and without trailing and leading pauses. Speech rate has been consistently identified as one of the major covariates of language proficiency and the features in this group have some of the highest correlations with the overall human score.
- Segmental quality features (6): These features measure how much the pronunciation of individual segments deviates from the pronunciation that would be expected from a proficient speaker. Features are derived from the confidence scores of the ASR system or acoustic scores of the forced alignment system. For instance, the normalized confidence score of the ASR system belongs to this group.
- Pause pattern features (9): These features capture pausing patterns in the response, such as mean duration of pauses, mean number of words between two pauses, and the ratio of pauses to speech.
- Prosody features (11): These features measure patterns of variation in the time intervals between stressed syllables as well as the number of syllables between adjacent stressed syllables (Zechner et al., 2011).
- Timing features (6): These features capture variation in the duration of vowels and consonants. This category includes features such as relative proportion of vocalic intervals or variability in adjacent consonantal intervals (Lai et al., 2013) as well as features which compare vowel duration to reference models trained on native speakers (Chen et al., 2009).

4 Experiment 1

4.1 Feature Generation

We first generated word hypotheses for each response in Table 1 using an ASR system. A gender independent acoustic model (AM) was trained on 800 hours of spoken responses extracted from the same English proficiency test using the Kaldi toolkit (Povey et al., 2011). The AM training dataset consisted of 52,200 spoken responses from 8,700 speakers. It was based on a 5-layer DNN with p-norm nonlinearity using layer-wise supervised backpropagation training. The language model (LM) was a trigram model trained using the same dataset used for AM training. This ASR system achieved a Word Error Rate of 23% on 600 held-out responses. Detailed information about the ASR system is provided in (Tao et al., 2016).

Next, we normalized both the prompt texts and the ASR-based transcriptions of the responses; all words were tokenized, and stop words and disfluencies were removed from the texts. The length of the original and the processed texts after removing stop words and disfluencies are summarized in Table 2.

The average lengths of the Independent prompts and the Integrated prompts were 41.0 and 341.6 words respectively; thus the Integrated prompts were approximately 8 times longer than Independent prompts.

Question type	Text normalization	Prompts				Responses			
		mean	STD	max	min	mean	STD	max	min
Independent	tokenized	41.0	15.5	100	20	97.3	22.1	173	11
	+stop word and disfluency removal	27.5	10.9	72	14	40.4	10.35	85	0
Integrated	tokenized	341.6	37.5	446	249	129.5	31.11	248	11
	+stop word and disfluency removal	230.3	26.1	302	168	53.1	13.7	107	0

Table 2: Descriptive analysis of the number of words in prompt texts and responses

After removing stop words and fillers, the texts were approximately $2/3$ of the original texts. The responses contained an average of 97 words for the Independent responses and 129 words for Integrated responses, but there were large variations across different responses. After the normalization process, the length of the responses was 40% of the original responses on average. The responses were shortened in larger proportion than the prompts because the responses contained disfluencies such as 'uh', 'um', which were removed.

From these normalized transcriptions, we created four content features as described in Section 3. In addition, 35 speech-driven features were generated using the original wave files and the same ASR word hypotheses.

4.2 Results

First, we conducted correlation analyses between features and human scores using the Scoring Model Train set. Table 3 presents Pearson correlation coefficients. For speech-driven features, the minimum and maximum for each group are presented.

	Independent	Integrated
Benchmark		
Response-based CVA	0.175	0.426
Prompt-based content features		
Prompt-based CVA	0.173	0.366
Averaged embedding	0.193	0.449
idf weighted embedding	0.240	0.455
Speech-based features		
Speech rate	(0.262, 0.524)	(0.315, 0.561)
Segmental quality	(0.168, 0.546)	(0.200, 0.586)
Pause pattern	(0.237, 0.494)	(0.243, 0.523)
Prosody	(0.147, 0.525)	(0.145, 0.558)
Timing	(0.248, 0.500)	(0.268, 0.527)

Table 3: Pearson Correlation Coefficients between features considered in this study and human scores for Independent and Integrated questions.

The correlations of content features were largely influenced by the question types. In general, the correlations for Integrated questions were substantially higher than those for Independent questions. The best performing feature was *idf* weighted embedding, and the correlation coefficients were 0.240 and 0.455, respectively.

In contrast to the content features, the differences between Independent questions and Integrated questions among the speech-based features were relatively small. There were large variations in the correlations among the features, and the lowest performing features in each group showed weak correlations with human scores, while the best performing features showed correlations over 0.50 with the exception of pause pattern group (0.494 for Independent questions). Among all features, the normalized acoustic model score in the Segmental quality group showed the best correlation with human scores with coeff-cients of 0.546 for Independent and 0.586 for Integrated.

We next considered whether adding content features to speech features improves performance of the automated scoring model. We trained multiple linear regression (MLR) models using both speech-driven and content features as the independent variables and the human score as the dependent variable. In order to compare the performance of the new features with the speech-driven features and investigate the impact of adding them to the existing model, we trained three models: speech (model based on 35 speech-driven features), content (model based on 3 prompt-based content features), and combination (model based on both speech-driven and content features, 38 features in total). In order to investigate the impact of the question types on the performance of content features, we trained each model for Independent and Integrated questions separately, yielding a total of 6 models. The models were trained on the Scoring Model Train partition using RSMTool (Madnani et al., 2017). Table 4 shows the performance of all models in terms of agreement between automated and human scores.

	Independent			Integrated		
	corr	wtkappa	RMSE	corr	wtkappa	RMSE
Speech	0.612	0.483	0.536	0.655	0.543	0.531
Content	0.270	0.150	0.653	0.522	0.413	0.600
Combination	0.613	0.483	0.536	0.663	0.551	0.526

Table 4: Correlations, weighted kappas and root mean squared error (RMSE) between the automated scores and human scores

We observed the following points:

- The performance of content models was strongly influenced by question type; the model performance for the Integrated questions was consistently better than that for the Independent questions.
- The speech models outperformed the content models for both question types.
- The combination of content features and speech-driven features (feature-level fusion) achieved a further improvement for Integrated questions; both correlations and weighted kappas increased approximately 0.008 in absolute value. Based on the Steigers Z-test for dependent correlations, this improvement was statistically significant at 0.01 level ($p < 0.01$).

4.3 Discussion

While adding content features lead to a statistically significant improvement in model performance for Integrated questions, this improvement was small and the scores from the two models were highly correlated with $r = 0.986$. Content features also received very low coefficients in the linear regression. However, the result is consistent with previous studies; Loukina and Cahill (2016) observed that content features such as unigrams or bigrams trained on question-specific sample responses achieved little improvement when combined with speech-driven features. They further argued that the majority of speakers who perform well along one dimension of language proficiency are also likely to perform well along other dimensions (see also Xi (2007), who reports similar results for human analytic scores). Consequently, the gain in performance from combining different systems is small or non-existent.

To explore this further, we conducted a further analysis using responses to Integrated questions and explored what types of responses benefited from the addition of content features. First of all, we observed that the content features were best at differentiating between low proficiency responses and the other responses. Figure 1 shows that the automated scores generated by the speech model consistently make distinctions across all score points as assigned by human raters. While for content models, the distinctions were clear for score points 1 and 2, but not for score points 3 and 4. The average automated scores for score point 3 and 4 were 2.73 and 2.88 respectively, and the difference was small.

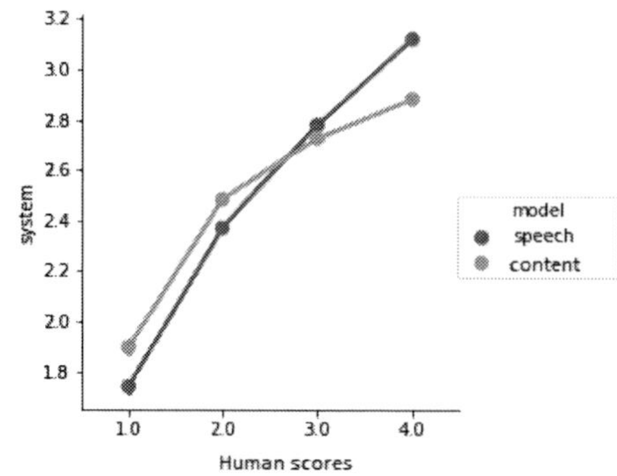

Figure 1: Average score predicted by the model based on speech features (blue) and content features (orange) for responses with different human scores.

Human score	1.0	2.0	3.0	4.0	All
N	1,548	12,721	16,054	2,661	32,984
Speech	0.860	0.523	0.387	0.925	0.531
Combination	0.836	0.518	0.389	0.912	0.526
Difference	-0.024	-0.005	0.002	-0.013	-0.005

Table 5: RMSE between the human scores and automated scores generated by the 'Speech' model, RMSE between the human scores and automated scores generated by the 'Combination' model, and the difference in RMSE between the two models.

We calculated RMSE between human scores and automated scores and averaged them for each human score level (see Table 5). Adding content features to speech features improved the model performance on low-proficiency responses: the decrease in RMSE was largest for score point 1 where it decreased from 0.86 to 0.84. Since less than 5% of the responses received score 1, this improvement had very little impact on overall model performance.

5 Experiment2

In Experiment 1, we found that new content features could reduce the automated score errors for the lowest score point. Based on this observation, we hypothesized that the new features could identify responses with substantial content issues and assign more accurate scores than the model based only on the speech-driven features for these responses. In order to examine this hypothesis, we artificially created a dataset with content issues by pairing responses with mismatched prompts for feature calculation.

5.1 Data

We first randomly selected 438 questions that did not overlap with the 147 questions used for the Scoring Model Train and Evaluation sets. Each question in our assessment was designed to elicit content that was substantially different from other questions, and therefore, mismatched responses have substantial content issues. For each question in the set of 147, we randomly selected 100 responses from the responses to the 438 questions. A total of $14,700$ responses ($4,900$ responses for Independent questions and $9,800$ responses for Integrated questions) were selected (hereafter, content-abnormality dataset). The average of the original human scores was 2.73 for Independent questions and 2.66 for Integrated questions. We did not re-score these responses as answers for the new question we randomly assigned. However, responses contained content inappropriate for the new questions, and the holistic proficiency scores were expected to be lower than the original scores due to this content issue.

5.2 Method

For each response in the content-abnormality dataset, we generated both speech-driven features and content features. For the content features, we did not use the original prompt text that elicited the response, but instead we used the new prompt text that was one of the 147 questions randomly selected as described in Section 5.1. Next, we generated three automated scores using the automated models described in Section 4.

5.3 Results

Table 6 presents the average of the automated scores of the content abnormality dataset.

	Independent	Integrated
Speech	2.70	2.63
Content	2.38	1.70
Combination	2.67	2.37

Table 6: Comparison of the automated scores for responses with content abnormality

The average scores of the speech models were 2.70 for Independent questions and 2.63 for Integrated questions, and they were similar to the average of the original human scores. In contrast, the average scores of the content models were lower than those of the speech models, and this trend was particularly salient for the Integrated questions. Finally, the models based on both features assigned lower scores than speech models on average, but the differences were relatively small; it was 0.03 for Independent questions and 0.26 for Integrated questions. This may be due to the low coefficients assigned to the content features in the linear regression models; the coefficients for Independent questions were lower than Integrated questions, and the difference of Independent questions was even smaller than that of Integrated questions.

Next, we further analyzed the automated scores for Integrated questions. Figure 2 shows the relationships between the automated scores and the original human scores.

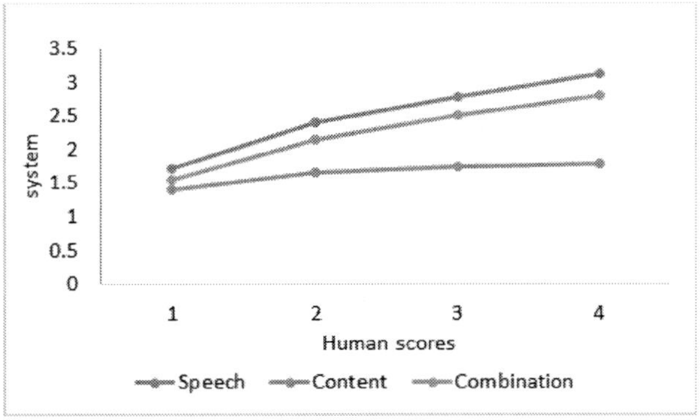

Figure 2: Average predicted scores of the models based on speech features (blue), content features (orange), and both feature sets (gray) conditioned by human scores.

In general, the automated scores of the content model were consistently lower than those of the other two models across all human score points. As the original human scores increased, the content scores also slightly increased, but the average scores for all score points were lower than 2.0. In contrast, as the original human scores increased, the scores of the speech model increased substantially, and the average scores except score point 1 were higher than 2.0. The high scores of the speech model was expected since it did not include any features to capture the content abnormality, and the automated scores may be inflated when the responses demonstrated good delivery skills (e.g., pronunciation and fluency) in spite of the content abnormality. In contrast, the content model consistently assigned lower scores for responses with the content abnormality. This result supports that the new content features are sensitive to the severe content issues and predict a more accurate score, which penalizes the content issues appropriately.

5.4 Discussion

Experiment 1 showed that the new content features improved the scoring accuracy for the responses with the lowest proficiency score. Furthermore, experiment 2 showed that these features could prevent the inflation of automated scores for responses with the critical content abnormality that caused a severe mismatch between delivery and content. However, we did not uncover evidence that new content features can improve score accuracy for responses with subtle and complicated content issues. These results are expected considering the nature of the proposed content features. The features were based on word unigrams and therefore may be able to make distinctions between responses with or without key concepts. However, they would not be able to differentiate whether the combination of these individual words conveys an appropriate meaning or not, which may be a key point for differentiating proficiency levels between the intermediate and advanced learners. Further qualitative review of a small set of responses was consistent with this conclusion: the scores of the content model were more accurate than those of the speech model when scoring responses with good coverage of the key words but low fluency. However, both models assigned high scores to responses that could be described as a continuous stream of mostly intelligible and relevant words but incoherent in terms of the content.

The holistic proficiency scores were not only based on the content, but raters also took into account other aspects of speaking proficiency, such as pronunciation, fluency, grammar, and vocabulary. However, if a test taker has comparable skills across all performance categories, then the score based on only one performance category may be comparable to the holistic proficiency score. For instance, if a response shows comparable skills for both the delivery and content, then the delivery-based score may be similar to the holistic proficiency score. If the majority of responses belong to this type, automated scores only measuring limited performance categories may show strong correlations with the experts' holistic proficiency scores. In this study, correlations between the automated scores based solely on speech features and the scores based on the combination of the content and speech features were very high, and two scores were seemingly identical. However, when scoring responses with severe content abnormality, the two scoring models showed different behaviors, and the scores based on both content and speech features correctly reflected the content abnormality. This result illustrates the importance of the coverage of the performance categories that automated scoring models assess; when scoring responses with mismatched proficiency levels in different performance categories, automated scoring systems assessing with limited coverage may show sub-optimal performance.

6 Conclusions

In this study, we proposed content features for an automated scoring system of non-native speakers' spontaneous speech. The content features calculated the similarity between the prompt texts and the ASR hypothesis of test responses, and therefore do not require any sample responses for each item during the training. The inclusion of new features achieved a small but statistically significant improvement for Integrated questions over the existing model based on speech-driven features solely assessing delivery skill. A further experiment using responses with artificially induced content abnormality showed that the inclusion of the new features may increase the validity of the automated scores by preventing the system from generating inflated scores for responses with good delivery skills but severe content issues.

Acknowledgements

We thank Abhinav Misra, Bruno James, Keelan Evanini, Klaus Zechner, Vikram Ramanarayanan, and three anonymous SemDeep reviewers for their comments and suggestions.

References

Suma Bhat and Su-Youn Yoon. 2015. Automatic assessment of syntactic complexity for spontaneous speech scoring. *Speech Communication*, 67:42–57.

Miao Chen and Klaus Zechner. 2011. Computing and evaluating syntactic complexity features for automated scoring of spontaneous non-native speech. In *Proceedings of the 49th Annual Meeting of the Association for Computational Linguistics 2011*, pages 722–731.

Lei Chen, Klaus Zechner, and Xiaoming Xi. 2009. Improved pronunciation features for construct-driven assessment of non-native spontaneous speech. In *Proceedings of NAACL*, pages 442–449.

Jian Cheng, Yuan Zhao D'Antilio, Xin Chen, and Jared Bernstein. 2014. Automatic assessment of the speech of young English learners. In *Proceedings of the Workshop on Innovative Use of NLP for Building Educational Applications*, pages 12–21.

Catia Cucchiarini, Helmer Strik, and Lou Boves. 2000. Quantitative assessment of second language learners fluency by means of automatic speech recognition technology. *The Journal of the Acoustical Society of America*, 107(2):989–999.

Keelan Evanini, Shasha Xie, and Klaus Zechner. 2013. Prompt-based content scoring for automated spoken language assessment. In *Proceedings of the Eighth Workshop on Innovative Use of NLP for Building Educational Applications*, pages 157–162.

Derrick Higgins, Jill Burstein, and Yigal Attali. 2006. Identifying off-topic student essays without topic-specific training data. *Natural Language Engineering*, 12(02):145–159.

Matt Kusner, Yu Sun, Nicholas Kolkin, and Kilian Q. Weinberger. 2015. From word embeddings to document distances. In *Proceedings of the 32nd International Conference on Machine Learning (ICML-15)*, pages 957–966.

Catherine Lai, Keelan Evanini, and Klaus Zechner. 2013. Applying rhythm metrics to non-native spontaneous speech. In *Proceedings of SLaTE*, pages 159–163.

Annie Louis and Derrick Higgins. 2010. Off-topic essay detection using short prompt texts. In *Proceedings of the NAACL HLT 2010 Fifth Workshop on Innovative Use of NLP for Building Educational Applications*, pages 92–95. Association for Computational Linguistics.

Anastassia Loukina and Aoife Cahill. 2016. Automated scoring across different modalities. In *Proceedings of the Workshop on Innovative Use of NLP for Building Educational Applications*, pages 130–135.

Anastassia Loukina, Nitin Madnani, and Aoife Cahill. 2017. Speech- and Text-driven Features for Automated Scoring of English Speaking Tasks. In *Proceedings of the First Workshop on Speech-Centric Natural Language Processing*, pages 67–77, Copenhagen, Denmark. Association for Computational Linguistics.

Nitin Madnani, Anastassia Loukina, Alina von Davier, Jill Burstein, and Aoife Cahill. 2017. Building better open-source tools to support fairness in automated scoring. In *Proceedings of the EACL Workshop on Ethics in Natural Language Processing*, pages 41–52.

Tomas Mikolov, Ilya Sutskever, Kai Chen, Greg S Corrado, and Jeff Dean. 2013. Distributed representations of words and phrases and their compositionality. In *Advances in neural information processing systems*, pages 3111–3119.

Jonas Mueller and Aditya Thyagarajan. 2016. Siamese recurrent architectures for learning sentence similarity. In *Proceedings of the Thirtieth AAAI Conference on Artificial Intelligence*, AAAI'16, pages 2786–2792. AAAI Press.

Paul Neculoiu, Maarten Versteegh, and Mihai Rotaru. 2016. Learning text similarity with siamese recurrent networks. In *Proceedings of the 1st Workshop on Representation Learning for NLP*, pages 148–157, Berlin, Germany, August. Association for Computational Linguistics.

Daniel Povey, Arnab Ghoshal, Gilles Boulianne, Lukas Burget, Ondrej Glembek, Nagendra Goel, Mirko Hannemann, Petr Motlicek, Yanmin Qian, Petr Schwarz, et al. 2011. The kaldi speech recognition toolkit. In *IEEE 2011 workshop on automatic speech recognition and understanding*, number EPFL-CONF-192584. IEEE Signal Processing Society.

Marek Rei and Ronan Cummins. 2016. Sentence similarity measures for fine-grained estimation of topical relevance in learner essays. In *Proceedings of the 11th Workshop on Innovative Use of NLP for Building Educational Applications*, pages 283–288.

Jidong Tao, Shabnam Ghaffarzadegan, Lei Chen, and Klaus Zechner. 2016. Exploring deep learning architectures for automatically grading non-native spontaneous speech. In *Acoustics, Speech and Signal Processing (ICASSP), 2016 IEEE International Conference on*, pages 6140–6144. IEEE.

Xinhao Wang, Keelan Evanini, and Su-Youn Yoon. 2015. Word-level f0 modeling in the automated assessment of non-native read speech. In *SLaTE*, pages 23–27.

Silke Witt and Steve Young. 1997. Performance measures for phone-level pronunciation teaching in CALL. In *Proceedings of the Workshop on Speech Technology in Language Learning*, pages 99–102.

Xiaoming Xi. 2007. Evaluating analytic scoring for the TOEFL® Academic Speaking Test (TAST) for operational use. *Language Testing*, 24(2):251–286.

Shasha Xie, Keelan Evanini, and Klaus Zechner. 2012. Exploring content features for automated speech scoring. In *Proceedings of NAACL*, pages 103–111.

Su-Youn Yoon, Suma Bhat, and Klaus Zechner. 2012. Vocabulary profile as a measure of vocabulary sophistication. In *Proceedings of the Seventh Workshop on Building Educational Applications Using NLP*, pages 180–189. Association for Computational Linguistics.

Su-Youn Yoon, Chong Min Lee, Ikkyu Choi, Xinhao Wang, Matthew Mulholland, and Keelan Evanini. 2017. Off-topic spoken response detection with word embeddings. *Proc. Interspeech 2017*, pages 2754–2758.

Klaus Zechner, Derrick Higgins, Xiaoming Xi, and David M. Williamson. 2009. Automatic scoring of non-native spontaneous speech in tests of spoken English. *Speech Communication*, 51(10):883–895.

Klaus Zechner, Xiaoming Xi, and Lei Chen. 2011. Evaluating prosodic features for automated scoring of non-native read speech. In *Proceedings of the IEEE Workshop on Automatic Speech Recognition & Understanding*, pages 461–466.

Automatically Linking Lexical Resources with Word Sense Embedding Models

Luis Nieto-Piña
University of Gothenburg
luis.nieto.pina@gu.se

Richard Johansson
University of Gothenburg
richard.johansson@gu.se

Abstract

Automatically learnt word sense embeddings are developed as an attempt to refine the capabilities of coarse word embeddings. The word sense representations obtained this way are, however, sensitive to underlying corpora and parameterizations, and they might be difficult to relate to word senses as formally defined by linguists. We propose to tackle this problem by devising a mechanism to establish links between word sense embeddings and lexical resources created by experts. We evaluate the applicability of these links in a task to retrieve instances of Swedish word senses not present in the lexicon.

1 Introduction

Word embeddings have boosted performance in many Natural Language Processing applications in recent years (Collobert et al., 2011; Socher et al., 2011). By providing an effective way of representing the meaning of words, embeddings facilitate computations in models and pipelines that need to analyze semantic aspects of language.

Based on their success, an effort has been concentrated in improving embedding models, from devising more computationally effective models to extending them to cover other semantic units beyond words, such as multi-word expressions (Yu and Dredze, 2015) or word senses (Neelakantan et al., 2014). Being able to represent word senses solves the problem of conflating several meanings of one polysemic word into a single embedding (Li and Jurafsky, 2015). Furthermore, having complete and accurate word sense representations brings embedding models closer to a range of existing, expert-curated resources such as lexica. Bridging the gap between these two worlds arguably opens a road to new methods that could benefit well-established, widely used resources (Faruqui et al., 2015; Speer et al., 2017).

This is the focus of the work we present in this article. We propose an automatic way of creating a mapping between entries in a lexicon and word sense representations learned from a corpus. By having an identification between a manual inventory of word senses and word sense embeddings, the lexicon obtains capabilities by which its entries can be manipulated as mathematical objects (vectors), while the vector space model receives support from a linguistic resource. Furthermore, by analyzing the disagreements between the lexicon and the embedding model, we can acquire insight into the shortcomings of their respective coverage. For instance, unlinked lexicon entries evidence those instances that the vector model is unable to learn, while unlinked word sense embeddings may suggest new usages of words found in the corpora. Being able to locate these cases opens the way towards improving lexica and embedding models. Automatic discovery of novel senses has been shown as a feasible and productive endeavor (Lau et al., 2012). In our evaluation we provide some insight into these situations: we use a mapping to calculate the probability that a word in a sentence from a corpus is an instance of an unlisted sense (i.e., not present in the lexicon.)

This mapping process, and some of its potential applications, are explained in detail in the following sections. Section 2 contains a description of the mapping mechanism Section 3 goes on to evaluate the performance of this mapping on finding instances of unlisted senses. We present our conclusions in Section 4.

Proceedings of SemDeep-3, the 3rd Workshop on Semantic Deep Learning, pages 23–29
Santa Fe, New Mexico, USA, August 20, 2018.

2 Model

2.1 Lexicon

A lexicon which lists word senses and provides relations between them is required; for instance, a resource that encodes these relations in a graph architecture, such as WordNet (Fellbaum, 1998).

We need to retrieve word senses related to any given target word sense in order to obtain a set of *neighbors* which put the target sense in context. This context will be used to compare it with sets of neighbors extracted from a word sense vector space for senses of the same lemma, and thus find the best match to establish a link.

In our experiments on Swedish data we use SALDO (Borin et al., 2013) as our lexicon. It is encoded as a network: nodes encode word senses, which are connected by edges defined by semantic *descriptors*: the meaning of a sense is defined by one or more senses, its descriptors. Among others, each sense has one *primary descriptor* (PD) and, in turn, it may be the primary descriptor of one or more senses. E.g., the PD of the musical sense of *rock* would be *music*, which would be the PD of *hard rock*. The PD network of SALDO traces back to a *root node* (which does not have a PD) and, thus, it has a tree topology. In general, senses with more abstract meanings are closer to the root, while more concrete ones are located closer to the leaves.

2.2 Word Sense Embeddings

Word sense embeddings allow us to create an analogy between semantic relatedness among words and geometric distance between their representations in a vector space. In particular, a word sense embedding model assigns multiple representations to any given word, each of which is related to a distinct word sense. For our purposes, we make use of Adaptive Skip-gram (Bartunov et al., 2016), an adaptation of the hierarchical softmax Skip-gram (Mikolov et al., 2013).

The hierarchical softmax model is described by its training objective: to maximize the probability of context words v given a target word w and the model's parameters θ:

$$p(v|w,\theta) = \prod_{n \in \text{path}(v)} \frac{1}{1 - e^{-\text{ch}(n) x_w^\top y_n}}, \tag{1}$$

where x_w are the input representations of the target words w, and the original output representations of context words y_n are associated with nodes in a binary tree which has all possible vocabulary words v as leaves; θ is the set of these representations as weights of the vector model. In this context, path(v) are the nodes n in the path from the tree's root to the leaf v, identified by ch(n) being -1 or 1 depending on whether n is a right or left child.

The Adaptive Skip-gram (AdaGram) model expands this objective to account for multiple word senses to be represented in the input vocabulary X. It does so by introducing a latent variable z that determines a concrete sense k of word w. The output vocabulary Y remains unchanged. This model uses a Dirichlet process (*stick-breaking representation*) to automatically determine the number of senses per word. They define a prior over the multiple senses of a word as follows:

$$p(z = k|w, \boldsymbol{\beta}) = \beta_{wk} \prod_{r=1}^{k-1} (1 - \beta_{wr}),$$

$$p(\beta_{wk}|\alpha) = \text{Beta}(\beta_{wk}|1, \alpha),$$

where $\boldsymbol{\beta}$ is a set of samples β from the Beta distribution and α is a hyperparameter. By combining this prior with a pre-specified maximum number of prototypes and a threshold probability, the model is able to automatically determine the number of word senses any given word is expected to have. The objective function that defines the AdaGram model is defined as follows:

$$p(Y, Z, \boldsymbol{\beta}|X, \alpha, \theta) = \prod_{w=1}^{V} \prod_{k=1}^{\infty} p(\beta_{wk}|\alpha) \prod_{i=1}^{N} \left[p(z_i|x_i, \boldsymbol{\beta}) \prod_{j=1}^{C} p(y_{ij}|z_i, x_i, \theta) \right], \tag{2}$$

Lexicon	Vector space
rock-1 'jacket'	*rock-b* (clothing)
rock-2 'rock music'	*rock-a*, *rock-c*, *rock-d*, *rock-e* (music)

Table 1: Example mapping for *rock*.

where V is the word vocabulary size, N is the size of the training corpus, C is the size of the context window, and $p(\beta_{wk}|\alpha)$ is the prior over multiple senses obtained via the Dirichlet process described above. The granularity in the distinction between word senses is controlled by α. A trained model produces representations for word senses in a D-dimensional vector space where those with similar meanings are closer together than those with dissimilar ones.

For the purposes of this work, we trained a word sense embedding model on a Swedish corpus (cf. Section 3.1) using the default parameterization of AdaGram: 100-dimension vectors, maximum 5 prototypes per word, $\alpha = 0.1$, and one training epoch. (See AdaGram's documentation for a complete list.)

2.3 Lexicon-Embedding mapping

Our goal is to establish a mapping between lexicographic word senses and embeddings that represent the same meanings. The approach we take is to generate a set of related word senses for each sense of any given word, both from the lexicon (via relations encoded in its graph's edges) and from the vector space (via cosine distance), to measure their relatedness and define mappings.

To obtain sets of neighbors from the lexicon, given any target word sense, any senses directly connected by an edge to the target's node is selected as a neighbor. In the vector space, nearest neighbors based on cosine distance are selected.

In order to measure relatedness using geometric operations we need to assign *provisional* embeddings to lexicographic neighbors in order to measure their distance to vector space neighbors. We do this by using AdaGram's disambiguation tool: given a target word and a set of context words, it calculates the posterior probability of each sense of the target word given the context words according to the hierarchical softmax model (Equation 1). The word in context is disambiguated by selecting the its sense with the highest posterior probability. (In our case, for any given sense, the rest of senses in the set act as context.)

We expect some lexicon-defined senses to not be present in the vector space and some word senses captured by the embedding model to not be listed in the lexicon. Additionally, the AdaGram model may create two or more senses for one word which relate to the same lexicographic sense. We address this by making the mapping 1-to-N to allow a lexicon sense to be linked to more than one sense embedding if necessary. Additionally, in order to make it possible for lexicon senses to be left unlinked, we propose to use a *false sense embedding* that acts as an attractor for those lexicon senses with weak links to real embeddings.

The mapping mechanism is shown in Algorithm 1. For each word in the vocabulary, a set of neighbors is generated for each of its senses in the lexicon and in the vector space. The vector representations of these neighbors are averaged, since averaging embeddings has been proven an efficient approach to representing multi-word semantic units (Mikolov et al., 2013; Kenter et al., 2016). A probability matrix $p \in [0,1]^{n \times m}$ is calculated by applying the softmax function to pairs of vectors. An extra column is added with scores generated by the softmax on zero-valued vectors to account for the false sense. A row in p represents the probability that each sense in the vector model corresponds to that row's lexicon sense, from which the maximum is obtained to establish a link. (A threshold ρ exists to avoid low-probability links.)

An example of the linking performed by this mechanism is shown on Table 1. According to the lexicon SALDO, the noun *rock* has two senses in Swedish: (1) 'jacket' and (2) 'rock music'. The word sense embedding model finds five different meanings for *rock*; upon inspection of their nearest neighbors, which give an indication of the closest senses to any particular meaning, four of them relate to the music sense (linked to *rock-2*) and one to items of clothing (linked to *rock-1*). As can be seen in Table 1, the

Algorithm 1 Mapping algorithm.

for all words w **do**
  /* *Lexicon neighbors* */
  $n \leftarrow$ #lexical senses of w
  $s_i \leftarrow i$th lexical sense of w, $i \in [1, n]$
  for all s_i **do**
    $a_i \leftarrow$ set of neighbors of s_i
    for all neighbor k in a_i **do**
      $v(a_{ik}) \leftarrow$ embedding for a_{ik}
    end for
  end for
  /* *Vector space neighbors* */
  $T \leftarrow$ max #senses per word
  $m \leftarrow$ #nearest neighbors (NN) per sense
  $z_j \leftarrow j$th sense embedding of w, $j \in [1, T]$
  for all z_j **do**
    $b_{jl} \leftarrow l$th NN of b_j, $l \in [1, m]$
  end for
  /* *Average neighbors* */
  for all i, j **do**
    $v(a_i) \leftarrow$ avg. vector over k
  end for
  for all j **do**
    $v(b_j) \leftarrow$ avg. vector over l
  end for
  /* *Mapping probabilities* */
  for all i, j **do**
    $p_{ij} \leftarrow \text{softmax}(v(a_i) \cdot v(b_j))$
    $p_{iN+1} \leftarrow \text{softmax}(\vec{0})$
  end for
  /* *Mapping* */
  for $j \in [1, T]$ **do**
    if prior$(s_j) > \rho$ **then**
      $r \leftarrow \text{indmax}_i(p_{ij})$
      if $r \neq N + 1$ **then**
        map s_r to z_j
      end if
    end if
  end for
end for

clothing-related meaning is linked to the sense meaning 'jacket', while the four music-related ones is linked to the sense meaning 'rock music'.

3 Evaluation

3.1 Training Corpus

For training the AdaGram model, we created a mixed-genre corpus of approximately 1 billion words of contemporary Swedish downloaded from Språkbanken, the Swedish language bank.[1] The texts were processed using a standard preprocessing chain including tokenization, part-of-speech-tagging and lemmatization. Compounds were segmented automatically and when the lemma of a compound word was not listed in SALDO, we used the lemmas of the compound parts instead. For instance, *golfboll* 'golf ball' would occur as a single lemma in the corpus, while *pingisboll* 'ping-pong ball' would be split into two separate lemmas.

3.2 Benchmark Dataset

For evaluation, we annotated a benchmark dataset. We selected five target lemmas for which we knew that the corpus contains occurrences of word senses that are unlisted in the lexicon. In addition, we selected four target lemmas that do not strictly have new word senses, but that tend to be confused with tokenization artifacts, named entities, or foreign words. Table 2 shows the selected lemma, an overview of the senses that are listed in the lexicon, as well as the most important unlisted senses.

For each of these nine target lemmas, we selected 1,000 occurrences randomly from the corpus. Two annotators went through the selected occurrences and determined which of them are instances of the senses present in the lexicon, and which of them are unlisted senses. A small number of occurrences were discarded because they were difficult for the annotators to understand.

[1] `http://spraakbanken.gu.se`

Lemma	Listed	Main unlisted
fet	'fat'; 'thick'	'cool'; emphasis
klient	'client' (customer)	'client' (application)
klubb	'club'	(night) 'club'
pirat	'pirate'	'pirate' (e.g. music)
sida	'side'; 'page'	'web page'
fil	'file'; 'row'; 'lane'; 'yogurt'	e.g. in *fil. dr.* 'PhD'
get	'goat'	foreign words
mus	'mouse'; 'pussy'	a cosmetic brand
sur	'sour'; 'grumpy'; 'soaked'	foreign words

Table 2: Selected target lemmas.

3.3 Experimental Settings

Given a mapping between lexicographic word senses and automatically discovered senses in a corpus, sentences from the benchmark dataset can be scored by their probability of containing an out-of-lexicon instance. A score is calculated using the linking probability between lexicographic sense y_j and vector model sense x_i, $P(y_j|x_i)$, and the probability of the AdaGram sense x_i in the context of the sentence ctx, $P(x_i|ctx)$:

$$P(y_j|ctx) = \sum_{i=1}^{T} P(y_j|x_i)P(x_i|ctx),$$

thus obtaining the probability of a particular lexicographic sense y_j given context ctx. The sum of all $p(y_j|ctx)$, $j \in [1, T]$, yields the probability that an instance contains one of the listed word senses. Our score, then, is calculated as the inverse probability:

$$\text{score} = 1 - \sum_{j=1}^{n} P(y_j|ctx). \tag{3}$$

The human annotations of the sentences are interpreted as the gold standard, and the scores as our model's classification output that can be used to rank the sentences from most to least probably containing an out-of-lexicon instance of a target word. We evaluate this classification using the Area Under the Receiver Operating Characteristic Curve (AUC). For reference, recall that the expected AUC of a random ranking is 0.5.

The potential of the automated mapping between a lexicon and an embedding model to help retrieve instances of word senses unlisted in the lexicon gives us a certain measure of the quality of this mapping. The recovery of instances of unlisted senses can only succeed if the mapping has successfully identified listed lexicon senses in the embedding model, leaving unlisted ones unlinked. On the other hand, failure to recover instances of unlisted senses can expose weaknesses in the automated mapping. (See Section 3.4 for an analysis of unsuccessful cases.)

3.4 Results

We apply the scoring and evaluation process explained above on the sets of sentences for each of the words selected for the benchmark dataset. Table 3 summarizes the results obtained. We observe a clear

Word	n	AUC
fet	976	0.76
klient	959	0.02
klubb	985	0.74
pirat	907	0.53
sida	985	0.69
Sub-avg.		0.55

(a) Unlisted senses.

Word	n	AUC
fil	982	0.87
get	954	0.98
mus	972	0.83
sur	967	0.96
Sub-avg.		0.91
Total avg.		0.73

(b) Spurious senses.

Table 3: AUC scores.

difference between the two types of lemmas: the model's performance is notably higher when the lemmas may be confused with tokenization artifacts, named entities or foreign words (Table 3b) than when the lemmas have meanings not listed in the lexicon (Table 3a). This is arguably due to the ability of the word sense embedding model to isolate spurious meanings in the vector space since these occurrences tend to be distributionally quite distinct from the standard uses. However, note that also for the case of unlisted meanings, the model generally improves over a random baseline.

The exception to this is the case of *klient*, where the listed sense is 'customer' and the new sense is 'client application'. Here, the ranking is upside down, as can be seen from the very low AUC value. The cause of this issue can be traced to the inability of the mapping algorithm to successfully link the only lexicographic sense to its corresponding vector space embedding. The neighbors of the AdaGram sense corresponding to the 'customer' sense tend to be legal terms, which are not connected to this sense in the lexicon. (Arguably, the legal use of 'client' could be seen as a separate sense.) Compare this to the case of *pirat*, which performs roughly at random (AUC ≈ 0.5), suggesting simply that the AdaGram model has not picked up the distinction between the senses, which makes it hard to solve the problem by simply changing the link, as would be the case with *klient*.

A straightforward way to address those cases in which the mapping fails to correctly establish a link would be to refine the way in which the word senses are represented at the time of linking. Our approach is to do this by averaging the embeddings of nearest neighbors, due to the simplicity and usual robustness of this operation. However, more complex approaches to combining embeddings have been demonstrated using, for example, weighted averaging (Arora et al., 2017), which could be adapted for our needs in this work.

4 Conclusion

We have presented an approach to automatically link lexicographic word senses with word sense embeddings by retrieving sets of senses related to the different meanings of a lemma and measuring the similarity between their vector representations. We argue that potential applications of such a system resides on those embeddings that cannot be linked to a lexicographic sense, as this could serve to suggest potential new entries to the lexicon, or to filter unlisted instances from a corpus. To illustrate this point, the evaluation of our system has been focused on its ability to retrieve instances assumed to belong to unlisted senses. Our system is able to identify such instances in many cases, as its performance in terms of AUC is above that of a random baseline. The performance is specially high in cases where the target lemma can be confused in the corpus with spurious meanings such as foreign words. In summary, our results indicate that establishing links between existing resources and embedding models has potential applications in NLP tasks which require formal lexicographic knowledge. In the future, we propose to examine ways to improve the current mapping system with improved neighbor representation approaches, as well as to investigate further possible uses, such as improving existing resources with data obtained from corpora.

Acknowledgements

This research was funded by the Swedish Research Council under grant 2013–4944.

References

Sanjeev Arora, Yingyu Liang, and Tengyu Ma. 2017. A simple but tough-to-beat baseline for sentence embeddings. In *International Conference on Learning Representations (ICLR)*.

Sergey Bartunov, Dmitry Kondrashkin, Anton Osokin, and Dmitry P. Vetrov. 2016. Breaking sticks and ambiguities with adaptive skip-gram. In *Proceedings of the 19th International Conference on Artificial Intelligence and Statistics (AISTATS)*.

Lars Borin, Markus Forsberg, and Lennart Lönngren. 2013. SALDO: a touch of yin to WordNet's yang. *Language Resources and Evaluation*, 47:1191–1211.

Ronan Collobert, Jason Weston, Léon Bottou, Michael Karlen, Koray Kavukcuoglu, and Pavel Kuksa. 2011. Natural language processing (almost) from scratch. *The Journal of Machine Learning Research*, 12:2493–2537.

Manaal Faruqui, Jesse Dodge, Sujay Kumar Jauhar, Chris Dyer, Eduard Hovy, and Noah A Smith. 2015. Retrofitting word vectors to semantic lexicons. In *Proceedings of the 2015 Conference of the North American Chapter of the Association for Computational Linguistics: Human Language Technologies*, pages 1606–1615.

Christiane Fellbaum, editor. 1998. *WordNet: An electronic lexical database.* MIT Press.

Tom Kenter, Alexey Borisov, and Maarten de Rijke. 2016. Siamese cbow: Optimizing word embeddings for sentence representations. In *Proceedings of the 54th Annual Meeting of the Association for Computational Linguistics (Volume 1: Long Papers)*, volume 1, pages 941–951.

Jey Han Lau, Paul Cook, Diana McCarthy, David Newman, and Timothy Baldwin. 2012. Word sense induction for novel sense detection. In *Proceedings of the 13th Conference of the European Chapter of the Association for Computational Linguistics*, pages 591–601. Association for Computational Linguistics.

Jiwei Li and Dan Jurafsky. 2015. Do multi-sense embeddings improve natural language understanding? In *Proceedings of the 2015 Conference on Empirical Methods in Natural Language Processing*, pages 1722–1732.

Tomas Mikolov, Ilya Sutskever, Kai Chen, Greg S Corrado, and Jeff Dean. 2013. Distributed representations of words and phrases and their compositionality. In *Advances in Neural Information Processing Systems*, pages 3111–3119.

Arvind Neelakantan, Jeevan Shankar, Alexandre Passos, and Andrew McCallum. 2014. Efficient non-parametric estimation of multiple embeddings per word in vector space. In *Proceedings of the 2014 Conference on Empirical Methods in Natural Language Processing (EMNLP)*, pages 1059–1069, Doha, Qatar, October. Association for Computational Linguistics.

Richard Socher, Eric H Huang, Jeffrey Pennin, Christopher D Manning, and Andrew Y Ng. 2011. Dynamic pooling and unfolding recursive autoencoders for paraphrase detection. In *Advances in Neural Information Processing Systems*, pages 801–809.

Robert Speer, Joshua Chin, and Catherine Havasi. 2017. Conceptnet 5.5: An open multilingual graph of general knowledge. In *AAAI*, pages 4444–4451.

Mo Yu and Mark Dredze. 2015. Learning composition models for phrase embeddings. *Transactions of the Association for Computational Linguistics*, 3:227–242.

Transferred Embeddings for Igbo Similarity, Analogy and Diacritic Restoration Tasks

Ignatius Ezeani **Mark Hepple** **Ikechukwu Onyenwe** **Chioma Enemuo**
Department of Computer Science,
The University of Sheffield, United Kingdom.
`https://www.sheffield.ac.uk/dcs`
`{ignatius.ezeani, m.r.hepple, i.onyenwe, clenemuo1}@shef.ac.uk`

Abstract

Existing NLP models are mostly trained with data from well-resourced languages. Most minority languages face the challenge of lack of resources - data and technologies - for NLP research. Building these resources from scratch for each minority language will be very expensive, time-consuming and amount largely to unnecessarily re-inventing the wheel. In this paper, we applied transfer learning techniques to create Igbo word embeddings from a variety of existing English trained embeddings. Transfer learning methods were also used to build standard datasets for Igbo word similarity and analogy tasks for intrinsic evaluation of embeddings. These projected embeddings were also applied to the diacritic restoration task. Our results indicate that the projected models not only outperform the trained ones on the semantic based tasks of analogy, word-similarity and odd-word identifying, but they also achieve enhanced performance on the diacritic restoration with learned diacritic embeddings.

1 Background

Most NLP systems are modelled with English data. One major challenge to adapting these systems for low resource languages is lack of good quality data. Such languages often rely on poor quality web-crawled data. In our case the target language is Igbo, a language spoken by over 30 million indigenes who live mainly in the south-eastern part of Nigeria but also in different parts of the world.

Inspite of the relatively large number of speakers, Igbo is critically low-resourced in terms of NLP research (Onyenwe et al., 2018). Recent efforts to develop resources for Igbo include the design of Igbo POS tagset (Onyenwe et al., 2014), and the tagset refinement (Onyenwe et al., 2015) as well as the development of Igbo POS-tagger (Onyenwe, 2017). Works are also on-going with its automatic diacritic restoration and lexical disambiguation (Ezeani et al., 2016) (Ezeani et al., 2017) and morphological segmentation (Enemouh et al., 2017).

1.1 Embedding Models

Word embeddings are generic semantic representations from corpus. It enhances the concept of distributional hypothesis (Harris, 1954) and count-based distributional vectors (Baroni and Lenci, 2010) and provides an alternative to the *one task, one model* approach. Their application areas span most NLP tasks and other fields such as biomedical, psychiatry, psychology, philology, cognitive science and social science (Altszyler et al., 2016). There are many approaches to training embedding models, however predictive (Mikolov et al., 2013a) and count-based (Pennington et al., 2014) models are very commonly used.

Ideally, a model trained in one language should capture similar semantic distribution in other languages. Since the large amount of data required to train such a model are not often available for low resource languages, transfer learning techniques could be used to project learned knowledge from one language to another.

Proceedings of SemDeep-3, the 3rd Workshop on Semantic Deep Learning, pages 30–38
Santa Fe, New Mexico, USA, August 20, 2018.

1.2 Transfer and Cross-lingual Learning

Transfer learning generally refers to the transfer of knowledge acquired in one domain in solving a problem in another domain. It is commonly applied when the target domain training data is limited (Weiss et al., 2016). With transfer learning we could take advantage of a parallel data that exist across languages in the form of word-aligned data, sentence-aligned data (e.g. Europarl corpus), document-aligned data (e.g. Wikipedia), lexicon (bilingual or cross-lingual dictionary) or even zero-shot learning with no parallel data.

In a survey of cross-lingual embedding models (Ruder, 2017), four different approaches were identified, *monolingual mapping* (Mikolov et al., 2013b; Faruqui and Dyer, 2014; Guo et al., 2015) which trains embeddings on large monolingual corpora and then linearly maps a target language word to its corresponding source language embedding vectors; *pseudo-cross-lingual* (Duong et al., 2016; Gouws and Søgaard, 2015; Xiao and Guo, 2014) which trains embeddings with a pseudo-cross-lingual corpus i.e mixing contexts from different languages; *cross-lingual* (Hermann and Blunsom, 2013; Hermann and Blunsom, 2014; Kočiský et al., 2014) trains embeddings on a parallel corpus constraining similar words to be close to each other in a shared vector space; *joint optimization* (Klementiev et al., 2012; Luong et al., 2015; Gouws et al., 2015) trains models on parallel or monolingual data but jointly optimise a combination of monolingual and cross-lingual losses. In this paper, we will adopt the projection approach described in (Guo et al., 2015).

2 Experimental Setup

Our experimental data consists of a collection of Igbo texts from the *Igbo Bible* and the translation of the *Universal Declaration of Human Rights*, two short novels: an Igbo version of *Eze Goes to School* and another Igbo novel *Mmadụ Ka A Na Arịa*. The pipeline has three stages. It starts with building the embedding models using training or projection methods (section 2.1). The next stage enhances the diacritic words with the embeddings of the its co-aligned English words (section 3.4.2). Lastly, the diacritic restoration is implemented as laid out in section 3.4.3.

In this experiment, we used only the Igbo-English parallel bible corpora, available from the *Jehova Witness* website[1], for the word alignment and projection of embedding models. The parallel data consist of 32,416 aligned lines of text. Additional data from the novels (3179 lines) and official documents (90 lines) make up the rest of the 35,685 lines of text with token sizes of 962,747 (without punctuations)[2] and vocabulary length 16,586 we used.

Although only 34% (328,591) of all tokens have diacritics, 54.8% (9,090) of vocabulary words are diacritic marked. There are 795 ambiguous *wordkeys*. A wordkey is a word stripped of its diacritics if it has any. Wordkeys could have multiple diacritic variants, one of which could be the same as the wordkey itself. Over 97% of the ambiguous wordkeys have 2 or 3 variants.

2.1 Building Igbo Embedding Models

In this work, we used both trained and projected embeddings for our tasks. We built the **igBible** embedding from the data using the Gensim *word2vec* Python libraries (Řehůřek and Sojka, 2010) with its default parmeters. We also used the **igWiki**, a pre-trained Igbo model from *fastText Wiki* project (Bojanowski et al., 2016), but it was removed due to its unstable performance across tasks which we could not resolve at the time of submission of this paper.

For the embedding transfer, we applied an alignment-based projection method (Guo et al., 2015). An Igbo-English alignment dictionary $A^{I|E}$ uses a function $f(w_i^I)$ that maps each Igbo word w_i^I to all its co-aligned English words $w_{i,j}^E$ and their counts $c_{i,j}$ as defined in Equation 1. $|V^I|$ is the vocabulary size of Igbo and n is number of co-aligned English words.

[1] `jw.org`

[2] There will be 1,138,036 in total with punctuations, symbols and digits

Model	Igbo Vocabs	Dimensions	Eng Vocabs	Train data
igBible	4968	300	–	902.5k
igEnBbl	4057	300	6.3k	881.8k
igGglNews	3046	300	3m	100bn
igWkNews	3460	300	1m	16bn
igWkSbwd	3460	300	1m	16bn
igWkCrl	3510	300	2m	600bn

Table 1: Igbo and English models: vocabulary, vector and training data sizes

$$A^{I|E} = \{< w_i^I, f(w_i^I) >\}; i = 1..|V^I| \\ f(w_i^I) = \{< w_{i,j}^E, c_{i,j} >\}; j = 1..n \tag{1}$$

The projection is formalised as assigning the weighted average of the embeddings of the co-aligned English words $w_{i,j}^E$ to the Igbo word embeddings $\mathbf{vec}(w_i^I)$ (Guo et al., 2015):

$$\mathbf{vec}(w_i^I) \leftarrow \frac{1}{C} \sum_{w_{i,j}^E, c_{i,j} \in f(w_i^I)} vec(w_{i,j}^E) \cdot c_{i,j} \tag{2}$$

where $C \leftarrow \sum_{c_{i,j} \in f(w_i^I)} c_{i,j}$

Using this projection method, we built 5 additional embedding models for Igbo:

- **igEnBbl** from a model we trained on the English bible.
- **igGNews** from the pre-trained *Google News*[3] *word2vec* model.
- **igWkNews** from *fastText* Wikipedia 2017, UMBC webbase corpus and statmt.org news dataset.
- **igWkSbwd** from same as **igWkNews** but with subword information.
- **igWkCrl** from *fastText* Common Crawl dataset

Table 1 shows the vocabulary lengths (*vocabs*), and the dimensions (*vectors*) of each of the models used in our experiments.

3 Model Evaluation

We evaluate the models on their performances on the following NLP tasks: *odd-words*, *analogy* and *word similarity* and diacritic restoration. As there are no standard datasets for these tasks in Igbo, we had auto-generate them from our data or transfer existing ones from English. Igbo native speakers were used to refine and validate instances of the dataset or methods used.

3.1 The *odd word*

In this task, the model is used to identify the *odd word* from a list of words e.g. *breakfast, cereal, dinner, lunch* $\rightarrow$ *"cereal"*. We created four simple categories of words Igbo words (Table 2) that should naturally be mutually exclusive. Test instances were built by randomly selecting and shuffling three words from one category and one from another e.g. *ọkpara, nna, ọgaranya, nwanne* $\rightarrow$ *ọgaranya.*

3.2 Analogy

This is based on the concept of analogy as defined by (Mikolov et al., 2013a) which tries to find y_2 in the relationship: $x_1 : y_1$ as $x_2 : y_2$ using vector arithmetic e.g $king - man + woman \approx queen$. We created pairs of opposites for some common noun and adjectives (Table 3) and randomly combined them to build the analogy data e.g. *di* (husband) – *nwoke* (man) + *nwaanyị*(woman) $\approx$ *nwunye*(wife) ?

[3]https://code.google.com/archive/p/word2vec/

category	Igbo words
nouns(family) *e.g. father, mother*	ada, ọkpara, nna, nne, nwanna, nwanne, di, nwunye
adjectives *e.g. tall, rich*	ọcha, ọgaranya, ogbenye, ogologo, oji, ọjọọ, okenye, ọma
nouns(humans) *e.g. man, woman*	nwaanyị, nwoke, nwata, nwatakịrị, agbọghọ, okorobịa
numbers *e.g. one, seven*	otu, abụọ, atọ, anọ, ise, isii, asaa, asatọ, itoolu, iri

Table 2: Word categories for *odd word* dataset

category	opposites
oppos-nouns	nwoke:nwaanyị, di:nwunye, okorobịa:agbọghọ, nna:nne, ọkpara:ada
oppos-adjs	agadi:nwata, ọcha:oji, ogologo:mkpụmkpụ, ọgaranya:ogbenye

Table 3: Word pair categories for *analogy* dataset

3.3 Word Similarity

We created Igbo word similarity dataset by transferring the standard *wordsim353* dataset (Finkelstein et al., 2001). Our approach used *Google Translate* to translate the individual word pairs in the combined dataset and return their human similarity scores. We removed instances with words that could not be translated (e.g. cell→*cell* & phone→*ekwentị*,7.81) and those with translations that yield compound words (e.g. situation→*ọnọdụ* & conclusion→*nkwubi okwu*,4.81)[4].

3.4 Diacritic restoration

The absence of proper diacritics in Igbo words causes ambiguities and may affect MT systems (Ezeani et al., 2016; Ezeani et al., 2017) (see Table 4). There are word-, grapheme-, and tag-based techniques (Francom and Hulden, 2013) for this task involving a huge amount of annotated data (Yarowsky, 1994; Yarowsky, 1999) which Igbo does not have. Techniques for low-resource languages (Mihalcea, 2002; Wagacha et al., 2006; De Pauw et al., 2011) but were not applied to Igbo. So far, works on Igbo used either too little data (Scannell, 2011), non-generic methods (Ezeani et al., 2016; Ezeani et al., 2017).

Statement	*Google Translate*	Comment
O ji *egbe* ya gbuo *egbe*	He used his **gun** to kill *gun*	wrong
O ji **égbè** ya gbuo **égbé**	He used his **gun** to kill **kite**	correct
Akwa ya di n'elu *akwa* ya	It was on the **bed** in his room	fair
Ákwà ya di n'elu **àkwà** ya	his **clothes** on his **bed**	correct
Oke riri *oke* ya	Her addiction	confused
Òké riri **òkè** ya	**Mouse** ate his **share**	correct
O jiri *ugbo* ya bia	He came with his *farm*	wrong
O jiri **ụgbọ** ya bia	He came with his **car**	correct

Table 4: Translation challenge for *Google Translate* (Ezeani et al., 2017)

3.4.1 Building the baseline n-grams

As our baseline, we used standard n-gram models with back-off and 10-fold cross validations. We focused on restoring only the ambiguous sets with a fair distribution of variants. To achieve this, we set a maximum threshold of 70% for any of the variants in a set i.e. if choosing the most common variant from a set gets 70% accuracy on that set, it is disqualified, leaving us with 215 (27%) of all 795 ambiguous wordkeys. Figure 2 shows that there is no significant improvement after the bigram model.

[4]An alternative considered is to combine the word e.g. *nkwubi okwu* → **nkwubi-okwu** and update the model with a projected vector or a combination of the vectors of constituting words.

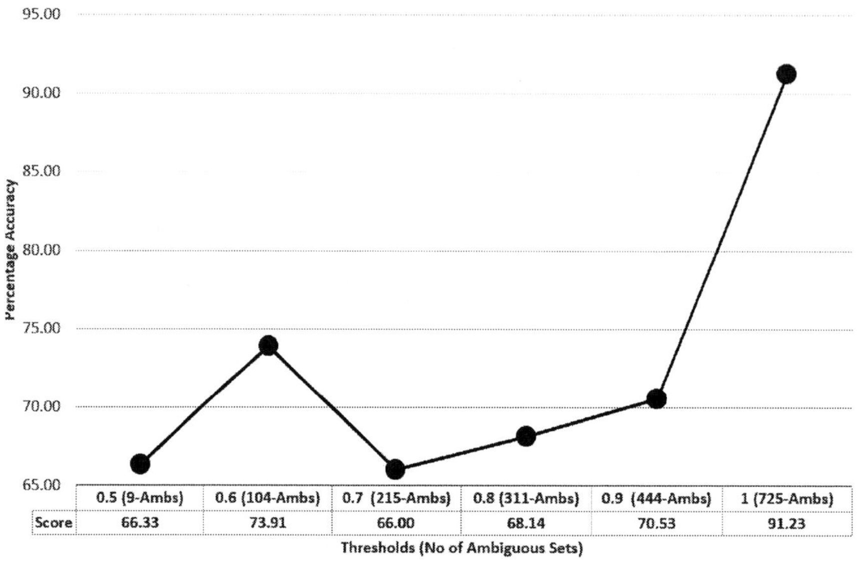

Figure 1: Average accuracy scores for all n-gram models: Thresholds [0.5 .. 1.0]

3.4.2 Deriving *diacritic* embedding models

The word **akwa** without context could mean **àkwá**(egg), **ákwà**(cloth), **ákwá**(cry/wail), **àkwà**(bed/bridge). The task is to ensure that the embedding for each of the variants of **akwa** exists in the model and is represented by the weighted combination of each of the most co-occurring words, mcw_v.

$$\mathbf{diac_{vec}} \leftarrow \frac{1}{|mcw_v|} \sum_{w \in mcw_v} vec(w) * w_c \tag{3}$$

where w_c is the 'weight' of w i.e. the count of w in mcw_v.

3.4.3 Diacritic restoration process

The restoration process computes the cosine similarity of the variant and context vectors and chooses the most similar candidate. For each wordkey, wk, candidate vectors, $D^{wk} = \{d_1, ..., d_n\}$, are extracted from the embedding model on-the-fly. C is defined as the context words (i.e. all the words in the same sentence) and vec_C is the context vector of C (Equation (4)).

$$\mathbf{vec_C} \leftarrow \frac{1}{|C|} \sum_{w \in C} vec_w \tag{4}$$

$$\mathbf{diac_{best}} \leftarrow \underset{d_i \in D^{wk}}{\mathbf{argmax}}\ sim(\mathbf{vec_C}, d_i) \tag{5}$$

4 Results and Discussion

Our results on the odd-word, analogy and word-similarity tasks indicate that the projected embeddings (Table 5, Figure 3) capture better general concepts and their relationships. This is not surprising as the trained model, **igBible**, and the one from its parallel English data, **igEnBbl** are too little and cover only religious data. Although **igWkSbwd** includes subword information which should be good for an agglutinative language like Igbo, these subword patterns are different from the patterns in Igbo. Generally the models from the news data, **igGNews, igWkNews**, did well on these tasks.

On the diacritic restoration task 6, the results compare the *basic* model (i.e. as trained or projected) with the *diac* (i.e. with variant vectors enhanced with the embeddings of their most co-occuring words.

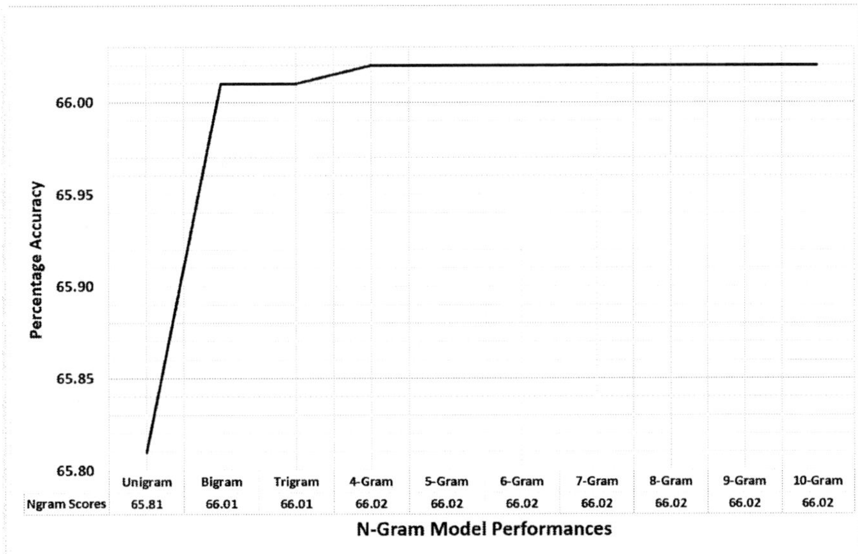

Figure 2: N-Gram accuracy scores for Threshold=0.7 (215) ambiguous sets

These models with semantic information, generally out-performed the n-gram models that capture more of syntactic details.

Also, compared to other projected models, **IgBible** and its parallel, **IgEnBbl** clearly did better on this task possibly it was originally trained with the same dataset and language of the task and its vocabulary directly aligns with that of **IgEnBbl**.

Clearly, the learned diacritic embeddings improved the performances of all the models which is expected as each variant is pulled to the center of its most co-occurring words.

	Odd-word	Similarity	Analogy	
Models	*Accuracy*	*Correlation*	*nouns*	*adjectives*
igBible	78.27	48.02	23.81	06.67
igGNews	**84.24**	60.00	64.29	**56.67**
igEnBbl	75.26	58.96	54.76	13.33
igWkSbwd	84.18	58.56	64.29	50.00
igWkCrl	80.72	**62.07**	78.57	21.37
igWkNews	81.51	59.69	**80.95**	50.00

Table 5: Trained and Project Embeddings on odd-word prediction

5 Conclusion and Future Research Direction

This work is part of the IgboNLP[5] (Onyenwe et al., 2018) project which aims at build a framework that can adapt, in an effective and efficient manner, existing NLP tools to support the development of NLP resources for Igbo. In this paper, we showed that, projected embedding models can outperform the one built with small language data on a variety of tasks. We also introduced a technique for learning diacritic embeddings which could be applied to the diacritic restoration task. Our next focus is to refine our techniques and datasets and train models with subword information as well as consider sense disambiguation task.

[5]See `igbonlp.org`

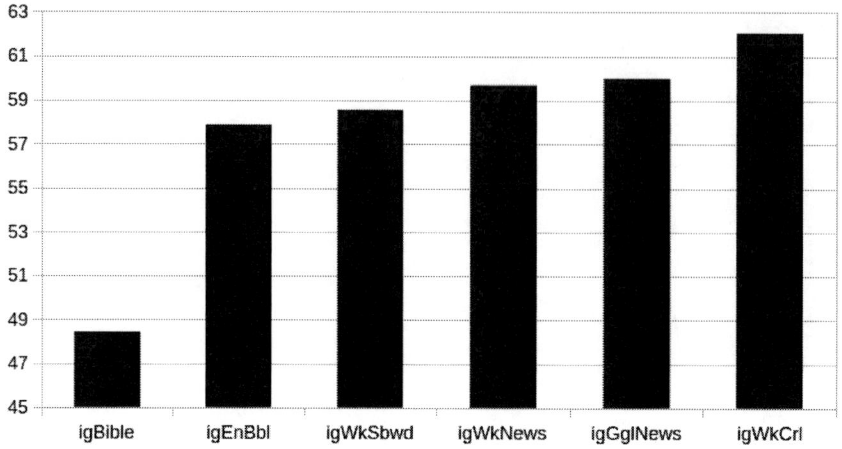

Figure 3: Worst-to-Best Word Similarity Correlation Performance

Baselines: *n*-gram models

	Unigram	*Best N-gram*
	65.81%	66.02%

Embedding models

	Accuracy		Precision		Recall		F1	
	Basic	Diac	Basic	Diac	Basic	Diac	Basic	Diac
igBible	69.28	**82.26**	61.37	77.96	61.90	**82.28**	57.19	**76.16**
igEnBbl	64.72	78.71	59.60	75.18	59.65	79.52	50.51	72.93
igGNews	57.57	74.14	32.20	72.50	49.00	74.56	19.06	62.47
igWkSbwd	62.10	73.83	13.82	73.81	47.64	74.03	10.65	66.62
igWkCrl	60.78	73.30	40.07	**78.02**	49.16	76.24	25.36	68.62
igWkNews	61.07	72.97	14.16	76.04	46.10	75.14	8.31	65.20

Table 6: Performances of Basic and Diacritic versions of the *Trained* and *Projected* embedding models on diacritic restoration tasks

References

Edgar Altszyler, Mariano Sigman, Sidarta Ribeiro, and Diego Fernández Slezak. 2016. Comparative study of lsa vs word2vec embeddings in small corpora: a case study in dreams database. *arXiv preprint arXiv:1610.01520*.

Marco Baroni and Alessandro Lenci. 2010. Distributional memory: A general framework for corpus-based semantics. *Computational Linguistics*, 36(4):673–721.

Piotr Bojanowski, Edouard Grave, Armand Joulin, and Tomas Mikolov. 2016. Enriching word vectors with subword information. *arXiv preprint arXiv:1607.04606*.

G. De Pauw, G. M. De Schryver, L. Pretorius, and L. Levin. 2011. Introduction to the Special Issue on African Language Technology. *Language Resources and Evaluation*, 45:263–269.

Long Duong, Hiroshi Kanayama, Tengfei Ma, Steven Bird, and Trevor Cohn. 2016. Learning crosslingual word embeddings without bilingual corpora. *arXiv preprint arXiv:1606.09403*.

C. Enemouh, M. Hepple, I. Ezeani, and I. Onyenwe. 2017. Morph-inflected word detection in igbo via bitext. *Widening NLP Workshop co-located with ACL 2017, Vancouver, July 30th 2017*.

Ignatius Ezeani, Mark Hepple, and Ikechukwu Onyenwe, 2016. *Automatic Restoration of Diacritics for Igbo Language*, pages 198–205. Springer International Publishing, Cham.

Ignatius Ezeani, Mark Hepple, and Ikechukwu Onyenwe. 2017. Lexical disambiguation of igbo through diacritic restoration. *SENSE 2017*, page 53.

Manaal Faruqui and Chris Dyer. 2014. Improving vector space word representations using multilingual correlation. In *Proceedings of the 14th Conference of the European Chapter of the Association for Computational Linguistics*, pages 462–471.

Lev Finkelstein, Evgeniy Gabrilovich, Yossi Matias, Ehud Rivlin, Zach Solan, Gadi Wolfman, and Eytan Ruppin. 2001. Placing search in context: The concept revisited. In *Proceedings of the 10th international conference on World Wide Web*, pages 406–414. ACM.

Jerid Francom and Mans Hulden. 2013. Diacritic error detection and restoration via part-of-speech tags. *Proceedings of the 6th Language and Technology Conference.*

Stephan Gouws and Anders Søgaard. 2015. Simple task-specific bilingual word embeddings. In *Proceedings of the 2015 Conference of the North American Chapter of the Association for Computational Linguistics: Human Language Technologies*, pages 1386–1390.

Stephan Gouws, Yoshua Bengio, and Greg Corrado. 2015. Bilbowa: Fast bilingual distributed representations without word alignments. In *International Conference on Machine Learning*, pages 748–756.

Jiang Guo, Wanxiang Che, David Yarowsky, Haifeng Wang, and Ting Liu. 2015. Cross-lingual dependency parsing based on distributed representations. In *Proceedings of the 53rd Annual Meeting of the Association for Computational Linguistics and the 7th International Joint Conference on Natural Language Processing (Volume 1: Long Papers)*, volume 1, pages 1234–1244.

Zellig S Harris. 1954. Distributional structure. *Word*, 10(2-3):146–162.

Karl Moritz Hermann and Phil Blunsom. 2013. Multilingual distributed representations without word alignment. *arXiv preprint arXiv:1312.6173.*

Karl Moritz Hermann and Phil Blunsom. 2014. Multilingual models for compositional distributed semantics. *arXiv preprint arXiv:1404.4641.*

Alexandre Klementiev, Ivan Titov, and Binod Bhattarai. 2012. Inducing crosslingual distributed representations of words. *Proceedings of COLING 2012*, pages 1459–1474.

Tomáš Kočiský, Karl Moritz Hermann, and Phil Blunsom. 2014. Learning bilingual word representations by marginalizing alignments. *arXiv preprint arXiv:1405.0947.*

Thang Luong, Hieu Pham, and Christopher D Manning. 2015. Bilingual word representations with monolingual quality in mind. In *Proceedings of the 1st Workshop on Vector Space Modeling for Natural Language Processing*, pages 151–159.

Rada F Mihalcea. 2002. Diacritics restoration: Learning from letters versus learning from words. In *International Conference on Intelligent Text Processing and Computational Linguistics*, pages 339–348. Springer.

Tomas Mikolov, Kai Chen, Greg Corrado, and Jeffrey Dean. 2013a. Efficient estimation of word representations in vector space. *arXiv preprint arXiv:1301.3781.*

Tomas Mikolov, Quoc V Le, and Ilya Sutskever. 2013b. Exploiting similarities among languages for machine translation. *arXiv preprint arXiv:1309.4168.*

Ikechukwu E Onyenwe, Chinedu Uchechukwu, and Mark R Hepple. 2014. Part-of-speech tagset and corpus development for igbo, an african language. *LAW VIII - The 8th Linguistic Annotation Workshop.*, pages 93–98.

Ikechukwu Onyenwe, Chinedu Uchechukwu, Mark Hepple, and Ignatius Ezeani. 2015. Use of Transformation-Based Learning in Annotation Pipeline of Igbo, an African Language. In *Recent Advances in Natural Language Processing, Hissar, Bulgaria.* Joint Workshop on Language Technology for Closely Related Languages, Varieties and Dialects.

Ikechukwu E Onyenwe, Mark Hepple, Uchechukwu Chinedu, and Ignatius Ezeani. 2018. A basic language resource kit implementation for the igbonlp project. *ACM Trans. Asian Low-Resour. Lang. Inf. Process.*, 17(2):10:1–10:23, January.

Ikechukwu Onyenwe. 2017. Developing methods and resources for automated processing of the african language igbo. *Doctoral dissertation.*

Jeffrey Pennington, Richard Socher, and Christopher Manning. 2014. Glove: Global vectors for word representation. In *Proceedings of the 2014 conference on empirical methods in natural language processing (EMNLP)*, pages 1532–1543.

Radim Řehůřek and Petr Sojka. 2010. Software Framework for Topic Modelling with Large Corpora. In *Proceedings of the LREC 2010 Workshop on New Challenges for NLP Frameworks*, pages 45–50, Valletta, Malta, May. ELRA. `http://is.muni.cz/publication/884893/en`.

Sebastian Ruder. 2017. A survey of cross-lingual embedding models. *CoRR*, abs/1706.04902.

Kevin P. Scannell. 2011. Statistical unicodification of african languages. *Language Resource Evaluation*, 45(3):375–386, September.

Peter W. Wagacha, Guy De Pauw, and Pauline W. Githinji. 2006. A Grapheme-based Approach to Accent Restoration in Gĩkũyũ. In *In Proceedings of the fifth international conference on language resources and evaluation*.

Karl Weiss, Taghi M Khoshgoftaar, and DingDing Wang. 2016. A survey of transfer learning. *Journal of Big Data*, 3(1):9.

Min Xiao and Yuhong Guo. 2014. Distributed word representation learning for cross-lingual dependency parsing. In *Proceedings of the Eighteenth Conference on Computational Natural Language Learning*, pages 119–129.

D. Yarowsky. 1994. A Comparison of Corpus-based Techniques for Restoring Accents in Spanish and French Text. In *Proceedings, 2nd Annual Workshop on Very Large Corpora*, pages 19–32, Kyoto.

D. Yarowsky, 1999. *Corpus-based Techniques for Restoring Accents in Spanish and French Text*, pages 99–120. Kluwer Academic Publishers.

Towards Enhancing Lexical Resource and Using Sense-annotations of OntoSenseNet for Sentiment Analysis

Sreekavitha Parupalli, Vijjini Anvesh Rao and Radhika Mamidi
Language Technologies Research Center, Kohli Center on Intelligent Systems,
International Institute of Information Technology, Hyderabad, India
{sreekavitha.parupalli, vijjinianvesh.rao}@research.iiit.ac.in
radhika.mamidi@iiit.ac.in

Abstract

This paper illustrates the interface of the tool we developed for crowd sourcing and we explain the annotation procedure in detail. Our tool is named as '*Parupalli Padajaalam*[1]' which means *web of words by Parupalli*. The aim of this tool is to populate the OntoSenseNet, sentiment polarity annotated Telugu resource. Recent works have shown the importance of word-level annotations on sentiment analysis. With this as basis, we aim to analyze the importance of sense-annotations obtained from OntoSenseNet in performing the task of sentiment analysis. We explain the features extracted from OntoSenseNet (Telugu). Furthermore we compute and explain the adverbial class distribution of verbs in OntoSenseNet. This task is known to aid in disambiguating word-senses which helps in enhancing the performance of word-sense disambiguation (WSD) task(s).

1 Introduction

OntoSenseNet is a lexical resource developed on the basis of Formal Ontology proposed by (Otra, 2015). The formal ontology follows approaches developed by Yaska, Patanjali and Bhartrihari from Indian linguistic traditions for understanding lexical meaning and by extending approaches developed by Leibniz and Brentano in the modern times. Based on this proposed formal ontology, a lexical resource for Telugu language has been developed (Parupalli and Singh, 2018) - OntoSenseNet for Telugu. The resource consists of words tagged with a primary and a secondary sense-types of verbs and sense-classes of adverbs. The sense-identification in OntoSenseNet for Telugu is manually done by experts in the field.

Sentiment analysis deals with the task of determining the polarity of text. To distinguish positive and negative opinions in simple texts such as reviews, blogs, and news articles, sentiment analysis (or opinion mining) is used. There are three ways in which one can perform sentiment analysis : document-level, sentence-level, entity or word-level. These determine the polarity value considering the whole document, sentence-wise polarity, word-wise in some given text respectively (Naidu et al., 2017).

2 Related Work

Extensive work has been done in the domain of sentiment analysis for English. We discuss few novel and relevant approaches here. (Esuli and Sebastiani, 2005) determines a new method for identifying the opinionated words (subjective terms) in the text based on the quantitative analysis of the glosses of such terms. (Gamon et al., 2005) present a prototype system for mining topics and sentiment orientation jointly from free text customer feedback. (Hatzivassiloglou and Wiebe, 2000) studies the role of adjectives in understanding the subjectivity. (Kaji and Kitsuregawa, 2007) aims at building a polarity lexicon from massive HTML documents. They propose a model to build a word-level polarity lexicon from the sentence-level polarity annotations.

(Gangula and Mamidi, 2018) created corpus "Sentiraama" for different domains like movie reviews, song lyrics, product reviews and book reviews in Telugu. Furthermore, his work aims to determine the performance of multi-domain sentiment analysis using reviews from several domains in Sentiraama

[1]https://github.com/Shreekavithaa/crowd-sourcing

Proceedings of SemDeep-3, the 3rd Workshop on Semantic Deep Learning, pages 39–44
Santa Fe, New Mexico, USA, August 20, 2018.

corpus. (Naidu et al., 2017) utilizes Telugu SentiWordNet on the news corpus to perform the task of Sentiment Analysis. (Mukku and Mamidi, 2017) developed a polarity annotated corpus where positive, negative, neutral polarities are assigned to 5410 sentences in the corpus collected from several sources.

(Abburi et al., 2016) proposes an approach to detect the sentiment of a song based on its multi-modality natures (text and audio). The textual lyric features are extracted from the bag of words. By using these features, Doc2Vec generates a single vector for every song. Support Vector Machine (SVM), Naive Bayes (NB) and a combination of both these classifiers are developed to classify the sentiment using the textual lyric features as a part of this work.

3 Crowd-sourcing Platform

Crowd-sourcing is an online, distributed problem-solving and production model that has emerged in recent years. Early user input can substantially improve the interaction design. Collecting input from only a small set of participants is problematic in many design situations. To address the above discussed problems, crowd-sourcing is widely adopted by research groups.

3.1 Add a Word

Any user can add a word to the resource. The user is prompted to enter the word, it's gloss and a sample sentence which shows the usage of the word. List of words received through this page are manually reviewed before adding to our resource.

3.2 User Profiling

As shown in Figure 1, any new user who wants to do the annotations must request the login credentials. This is necessary to control the access and avoid unauthentic annotations of the resource. Users are requested to submit their information such as name, email ID, profession, educational background and a score is assigned to the user based on his/her proficiency in Telugu. Score is assigned based on their responses to few questions asked in the request credentials form. This score is used in resolving the conflicts that may arise during annotation. For example, if any word has different tags given by different annotators, the tag given by the annotator with higher score is considered to be accurate. Once the profile is verified, the login credentials are sent to the user through an email.

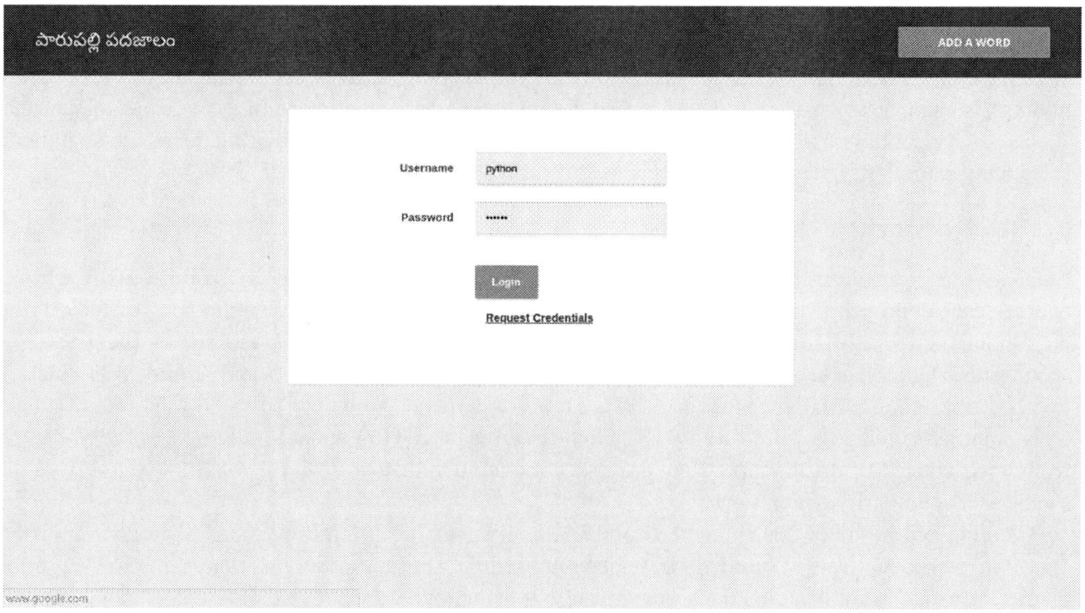

Figure 1: Login page

3.3 Annotations

We use this tool to perform two kinds of annotations that are discussed as the part of this thesis.

3.3.1 Ontological Sense Annotations

After logging in, all the users are requested to go through the annotation guidelines before performing the task. These annotation guidelines clearly explain the sense-types and sense-classes proposed. The user is shown a word, its meanings and is prompted to choose the appropriate primary and secondary sense-type of the verbs through the list of options available in the drop down menu as shown in figure 2. Along with the 7 sense-type tags, the user has the liberty to tag a word(verb) as 'uncertain' in case of an unclear judgment. The list of uncertain words are added to the list of the word to-be annotated. Words which are tagged to be uncertain consistently are reviewed and removed from the resource. Similar scheme is followed for the adjectives. In case of adjectives, the user could choose to tag the word as any of the 6 defined sense-types or tag the word as 'uncertain'.

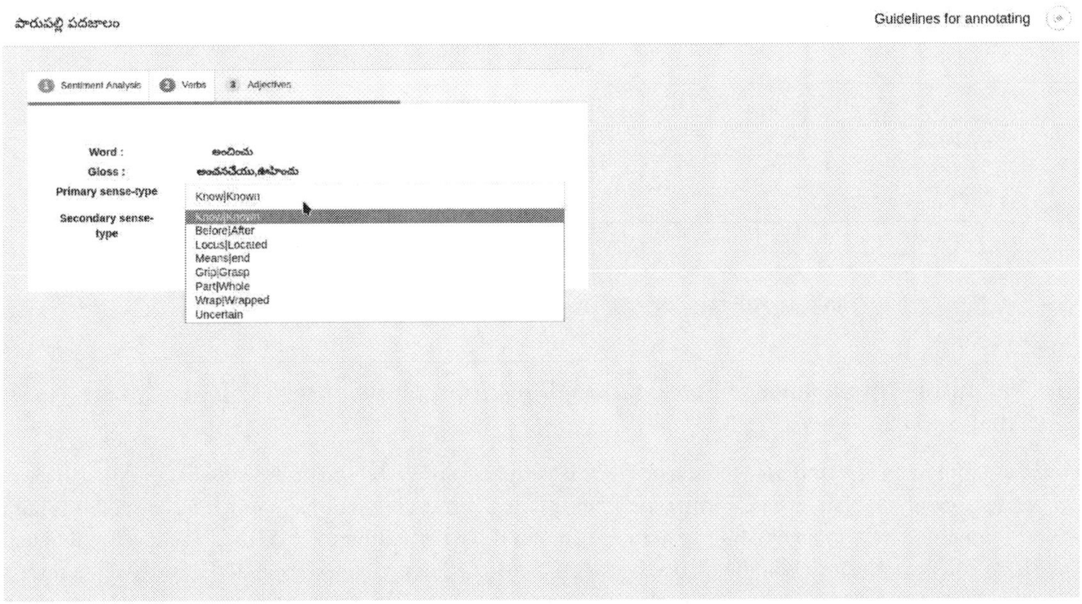

Figure 2: Verb annotation interface with options given to the user

3.3.2 Sentiment Polarity Annotations

In case of polarity annotations, sentiment polarities are classified into 4 labels : positive, negative, neutral and uncertain. Positive and negative labels are given in case of positive and negative sentiments in the word respectively. Uncertain/ambiguous label is given to words which acquire sentiment based on the words it is used along with or it's position in a sentence. Neutral label is given when the word has no sentiment in it.

4 Adverbial Class Distribution of Verbs

We have extracted all the Verb-Adverb and Adverb-Verb pairs from the Telugu Wikipedia. In order to acquire these patterns we performed the task of POS tagging[2] on Wikipedia corpus. From the extracted pairs, we noticed that there are comparatively more Adverb-Verb pairs than Verb-Adverb pairs which align with the structure of Telugu language(RJ et al., 2008). 400 verbs and 445 adverbs are annotated according to the formal ontology that is discussed in (Parupalli and Singh, 2018). These words formed

[2] https://bitbucket.org/sivareddyg/telugu-part-of-speech-tagger

about 2000 Verb-Adverb and Adverb-Verb pairs. Our aim is to study the adverbial class distribution of verbs in Telugu. (Otra, 2015) proves that such annotations help in disambiguating the word senses thus result in improved word-sense disambiguation (WSD) task(s). This is one of the major applications of OntoSenseNet.

In table 1, we show the adverbial class distribution of verbs in Verb-Adverb and Adverb-Verb pairs. Adverbial sense-classes are labeled as columns and sense-types of verbs are labeled as rows. Any cell in the table represents the percentage of a 'sense-class' of adverbs that modify a particular 'sense-type' of verbs. For example : Column-1 of 1 means 20.0% of 'spatial'; 13.6% of 'temporal'; 18.8% of 'force' and 24.4% of 'measure' sense-classed of adverbs modify 'to know' sense-type of verbs. This shows that majority of the 'to know' verbs are primarily modified by adverbs with 'measure' sense-class. For example : *cl anipicidi* (feel immensely). 'To move', 'to do' verbs are primarily modified by 'spatial', 'force' sense-class of adverbs respectively. Examples are *nerug mlutu*(talk in a straight forward manner), *emoanalg locistu* (think emotionally). 'Temporal' sense-class of adverbs can modify all the sense-types of verbs. 'To be' sense-type of verbs is also significantly modified by 'force' sense-class of adverbs. However, 'temporal' and 'measure' sense-classes also seem to show comparable performance in modifying 'to be' sense-type. We can find many such examples in Telugu language.

	To Know	To Move	To Do	To Have	To Be	To Cut	To Bound
Spatial	20.0 %	28.5%	20 %	9.5 %	9.5 %	8.5%	4.0 %
Temporal	13.6 %	22.0 %	14.6%	20.5%	20.5 %	4.4%	4.4 %
Force	18.8 %	21.5 %	22.2%	7.2%	22.9%	6.0%	4.1%
Measure	24.4%	16.5 %	19.5%	5.2%	20.3 %	7.5%	3.8%

Table 1: Adverb Sense-Class Distribution in Verb-Adverb pairs

5 Validating Importance of Sense-annotations from OntoSenseNet on Sentiment Analysis.

In an attempt to understand how the sense-type classification of verbs and sense-classes for adverbs could affect sentiment analysis, we perform experiments using sense-annotations from OntoSenseNet(Telugu) as additional features to an existing system as discussed in (Parupalli et al., 2018). We develop a benchmark Word2Vec approach which utilizes averaged word vectors generated from all the words in a review, adopted from Sentiraama corpus(Gangula and Mamidi, 2018). The constructed review vector is used to determine the benchmark accuracy for sentiment classification. To validate the importance of word-level annotations, the following features are added to our review vectors:

5.1 Word-level Polarity Features

SentiWordNet(Das and Gambäck, 2012; Das and Bandyopadhyay, 2010; Amitava and Bandyopadhyay, 2011) is a lexical resource with sentiment polarity annotations. It has 4076 negative and 2135 positive unigrams. (Parupalli et al., 2018) shows the importance of word-level annotations on sentiment analysis task. The features they consider are number of positive unigrams from SentiWordNet + their annotated data, number of negative unigrams from SentiWordNet + their annotated data, number of positive bigrams, number of negative bigrams from Sentiraama (Gangula and Mamidi, 2018).

5.2 Additional Features from OntoSenseNet

Utilizing the sense-annotations from OntoSenseNet resource, we added the following features to our review vectors:

- Verbs from OntoSenseNet are annotated with 7 sense-type tags namely- To Know, To Move, To Do, To Have, To Be, To Cut, To Bound. We add the frequency of these sense-types in the review, to the averaged word vector of the review. This results in addition of 7 features to the review (feature) vector.

- Adverbs from OntoSenseNet are annotated with 4 sense-class tags namely- Spatial, Temporal, Force, Measure adverbs in the review. We add the frequency of these sense-class tags to the review vector. Along with features from obtained from verbs, we add these 4 features. On the whole, we get 11 additional features from OntoSenseNet resource.

5.3 Results

2 shows results of our experiments with various classifiers. K-Nearest neighbor (KNN) classifier shows a huge drop in accuracy after inclusion of the new features. This might be because KNN doesn't differentiate between the features and holds all with equal importance for classification. Hence, it fails to ignore the probable noisy features among the newly added ones. On the other hand, Random Forest (RF) classifier keeps learning from additional features and is good at ignoring the noisy ones. We observe an interesting trend in the accuracies i.e. performance of Linear SVM keeps decreasing and at the same time performance of Gaussian SVM keeps increasing. This shows loss of linear separability. On the whole, we find Neural Network (NN) to be best performing classifier when averaged over repeated trials. However, repeated trials of the experiment show high variance. 3 shows in detail the precision, recall, and f1-scores of Neural Network's performance with two hidden layers of size 100 and 25 and input vectors of 200 dimensions without additional features. The increment in accuracy over addition of features extracted from OntoSenseNet validate our hypothesis that OntoSenseNet *does* contain semantic knowledge valuable to the task of sentiment analysis.

	Word2Vec	**+word-level polarity features**	**+ OntoSenseNet features**	**+ Both**
Linear SVM	81.59 %	70.64%	78.10 %	76.11 %
Gaussian SVM	48.25 %	67.66 %	66.16%	73.63%
Random Forest	74.62 %	75.12 %	77.61%	75.62%
Neural Network	81.09%	75.62 %	**83.08%**	81.09%
K-Nearest Neighbor	81.09%	62.68 %	65.17%	68.15%

Table 2: Accuracy for various classifier with different features.

	Word2Vec	**+word-level polarity features**	**+ OntoSenseNet features**	**+ Both**
Precision	0.820	0.760	0.833	0.811
Recall	0.813	0.753	0.829	0.811
F-Measure	0.810	0.753	0.829	0.810

Table 3: Precision, Recall and F1-scores for Neural Network with different features.

6 Conclusion

This paper presents the tool developed for crowd-sourcing the annotations that are yet to-be done. In the development of OntoSenseNet only 1673 adjectives out of 11,000 were annotated. Rest of these adjectives will be annotated through crowd-sourcing approach. Additional verbs extracted from WordNet also need annotations to be done. In sentiment analysis task, most of the unigram annotations are done through crowd-sourcing approach. Before this tool is developed, annotations are crowd-sourced using Amazon Mechanical Turk (MTurk) [3]. The bigrams (verb, adverb pairs) discussed in section 4 are yet to be annotated through the tool. The adverbial class distribution of verbs is extracted from Telugu Wikipedia that is aimed to improvise WSD tasks. We present the insights obtained from the statistics. We validate our hypothesis that features extracted from OntoSenseNet carry relevant information that is useful for sentiment analysis through machine learning approaches.

[3] https://www.mturk.com

7 Acknowledgments

I want to thank Abhilash Reddy for his help in developing the crowd sourcing tool. I want to thank Mrs. Vijaya Lakshmi Kiran Kumar for her continuous support and encouragement.

References

[Abburi et al.2016] Harika Abburi, Eswar Sai Akhil Akkireddy, Suryakanth Gangashetti, and Radhika Mamidi. 2016. Multimodal sentiment analysis of telugu songs. In *SAAIP@ IJCAI*, pages 48–52.

[Amitava and Bandyopadhyay2011] Das Amitava and Sivaji Bandyopadhyay. 2011. Dr sentiment knows everything. In *Proceedings of the 49th annual meeting of the association for computational linguistics, human language technologies, systems demonstrations, Association for Computational Linguistics.*

[Das and Bandyopadhyay2010] Amitava Das and Sivaji Bandyopadhyay. 2010. Sentiwordnet for indian languages. In *Proceedings of the Eighth Workshop on Asian Language Resouces*, pages 56–63.

[Das and Gambäck2012] Amitava Das and Björn Gambäck. 2012. Sentimantics: conceptual spaces for lexical sentiment polarity representation with contextuality. In *Proceedings of the 3rd Workshop in Computational Approaches to Subjectivity and Sentiment Analysis*, pages 38–46. Association for Computational Linguistics.

[Esuli and Sebastiani2005] Andrea Esuli and Fabrizio Sebastiani. 2005. Determining the semantic orientation of terms through gloss classification. In *Proceedings of the 14th ACM international conference on Information and knowledge management*, pages 617–624. ACM.

[Gamon et al.2005] Michael Gamon, Anthony Aue, Simon Corston-Oliver, and Eric Ringger. 2005. Pulse: Mining customer opinions from free text. In *international symposium on intelligent data analysis*, pages 121–132. Springer.

[Gangula and Mamidi2018] Rama Rohit Reddy Gangula and Radhika Mamidi. 2018. Resource creation towards automated sentiment analysis in telugu (a low resource language) and integrating multiple domain sources to enhance sentiment prediction. In Nicoletta Calzolari (Conference chair), Khalid Choukri, Christopher Cieri, Thierry Declerck, Sara Goggi, Koiti Hasida, Hitoshi Isahara, Bente Maegaard, Joseph Mariani, Hlne Mazo, Asuncion Moreno, Jan Odijk, Stelios Piperidis, and Takenobu Tokunaga, editors, *Proceedings of the Eleventh International Conference on Language Resources and Evaluation (LREC 2018)*, Paris, France, may. European Language Resources Association (ELRA).

[Hatzivassiloglou and Wiebe2000] Vasileios Hatzivassiloglou and Janyce M Wiebe. 2000. Effects of adjective orientation and gradability on sentence subjectivity. In *Proceedings of the 18th conference on Computational linguistics-Volume 1*, pages 299–305. Association for Computational Linguistics.

[Kaji and Kitsuregawa2007] Nobuhiro Kaji and Masaru Kitsuregawa. 2007. Building lexicon for sentiment analysis from massive collection of html documents. In *Proceedings of the 2007 Joint Conference on Empirical Methods in Natural Language Processing and Computational Natural Language Learning (EMNLP-CoNLL).*

[Mukku and Mamidi2017] Sandeep Sricharan Mukku and Radhika Mamidi. 2017. Actsa: Annotated corpus for telugu sentiment analysis. In *Proceedings of the First Workshop on Building Linguistically Generalizable NLP Systems*, pages 54–58.

[Naidu et al.2017] Reddy Naidu, Santosh Kumar Bharti, Korra Sathya Babu, and Ramesh Kumar Mohapatra. 2017. Sentiment analysis using telugu sentiwordnet.

[Otra2015] Spandana Otra. 2015. *TOWARDS BUILDING A LEXICAL ONTOLOGY RESOURCE BASED ON INTRINSIC SENSES OF WORDS*. Ph.D. thesis, International Institute of Information Technology Hyderabad.

[Parupalli and Singh2018] Sreekavitha Parupalli and Navjyoti Singh. 2018. Enrichment of ontosensenet: Adding a sense-annotated telugu lexicon. *arXiv preprint arXiv:1804.02186.*

[Parupalli et al.2018] S. Parupalli, V. Anvesh Rao, and R. Mamidi. 2018. BCSAT : A Benchmark Corpus for Sentiment Analysis in Telugu Using Word-level Annotations. *ArXiv e-prints*, July.

[RJ et al.2008] Rama Sree RJ, Madhu Murthy KV, et al. 2008. Assessment and development of pos tag set for telugu. In *Proceedings of the 6th Workshop on Asian Language Resources.*

Knowledge Representation with Conceptual Spaces

Steven Schockaert
School of Computer Science and Informatics, Cardiff University, UK
SchockaertS1@cardiff.ac.uk

Bio

Steven Schockaert is a professor at Cardiff University. His current research interests include commonsense reasoning, interpretable machine learning, vagueness and uncertainty modelling, representation learning, and information retrieval. He holds an ERC Starting Grant, and has previously been supported by funding from the Leverhulme Trust, EPSRC, and FWO, among others. He was the recipient of the 2008 ECCAI Doctoral Dissertation Award and the IBM Belgium Prize for Computer Science. He is on the board of directors of EurAI, on the editorial board of Artificial Intelligence and an area editor for Fuzzy Sets and Systems. He was PC co-chair of SUM 2016 and the general chair of UKCI 2017.

Abstract

Entity embeddings are vector space representations of a given domain of interest. They are typically learned from text corpora (possibly in combination with any available structured knowledge), based on the intuition that similar entities should be represented by similar vectors. The usefulness of such entity embeddings largely stems from the fact that they implicitly encode a rich amount of knowledge about the considered domain, beyond mere similarity. In an embedding of movies, for instance, we may expect all movies from a given genre to be located in some low-dimensional manifold. This is particularly useful in supervised learning settings, where it may e.g. allow neural movie recommenders to base predictions on the genre of a movie, without that genre having to be specified explicitly for each movie, or without even the need to specify that the genre of a movie is a property that may have predictive value for the considered task. In unsupervised settings, however, such implicitly encoded knowledge cannot be leveraged.

Conceptual spaces, as proposed by Grdenfors, are similar to entity embeddings, but provide more structure. In conceptual spaces, among others, dimensions are interpretable and grouped into facets, and properties and concepts are explicitly modelled as (vague) regions. Thanks to this additional structure, conceptual spaces can be used as a knowledge representation framework, which can also be effectively exploited in unsupervised settings. Given a conceptual space of movies, for instance, we are able to answer queries that ask about similarity w.r.t. a particular facet (e.g. movies which are cinematographically similar to Jurassic Park), that refer to a given feature (e.g. movies which are scarier than Jurassic Park but otherwise similar), or that refer to particular properties or concepts (e.g. thriller from the 1990s with a dinosaur theme). Compared to standard entity embeddings, however, conceptual spaces are more challenging to learn in a purely data-driven fashion. In this talk, I will give an overview of some approaches for learning such representations that have recently been developed within the context of the FLEXILOG project.

Proceedings of SemDeep-3, the 3rd Workshop on Semantic Deep Learning, page 45
Santa Fe, New Mexico, USA, August 20, 2018.

Knowledge Representation and Extraction at Scale

Christos Christodoulopoulos
Amazon Research, Cambridge, UK
chrchrs@amazon.co.uk

Bio

Christos Christodoulopoulos is a Research Scientist at Amazon Research Cambridge (UK), working on knowledge extraction and verification. He got his PhD at the University of Edinburgh, where he studied the underlying structure of syntactic categories across languages. Before joining Amazon, he was a post-doctoral researcher at the University of Illinois working on semantic role labeling and psycholinguistic models of language acquisition. He has experience in science communication including giving public talks and producing a science podcast.

Abstract

These days, most general knowledge question-answering systems rely on large-scale knowledge bases comprising billions of facts about millions of entities. Having a structured source of semantic knowledge means that we can answer questions involving single static facts (e.g. "Who was the 8th president of the US?") or dynamically generated ones (e.g. "How old is Donald Trump?"). More importantly, we can answer questions involving multiple inference steps ("Is the queen older than the president of the US?").

In this talk, I'm going to be discussing some of the unique challenges that are involved with building and maintaining a consistent knowledge base for Alexa, extending it with new facts and using it to serve answers in multiple languages. I will focus on three recent projects from our group. First, a way of measuring the completeness of a knowledge base, that is based on usage patterns. The definition of the usage of the KB is done in terms of the relation distribution of entities seen in question-answer logs. Instead of directly estimating the relation distribution of individual entities, it is generalized to the "class signature" of each entity. For example, users ask for baseball players' height, age, and batting average, so a knowledge base is complete (with respect to baseball players) if every entity has facts for those three relations.

Second, an investigation into fact extraction from unstructured text. I will present a method for creating distant (weak) supervision labels for training a large-scale relation extraction system. I will also discuss the effectiveness of neural network approaches by decoupling the model architecture from the feature design of a state-of-the-art neural network system. Surprisingly, a much simpler classifier trained on similar features performs on par with the highly complex neural network system (at 75x reduction to the training time), suggesting that the features are a bigger contributor to the final performance.

Finally, I will present the Fact Extraction and VERification (FEVER) dataset and challenge. The dataset comprises more than 185,000 human-generated claims extracted from Wikipedia pages. False claims were generated by mutating true claims in a variety of ways, some of which were meaning-altering. During the verification step, annotators were required to label a claim for its validity and also supply full-sentence textual evidence from (potentially multiple) Wikipedia articles for the label. With FEVER, we aim to help create a new generation of transparent and interprable knowledge extraction systems.

Proceedings of SemDeep-3, the 3rd Workshop on Semantic Deep Learning, page 46
Santa Fe, New Mexico, USA, August 20, 2018.

Author Index

Association for Computational Linguistics
209 N. Eighth Street
Stroudsburg, Pennsylvania 18360

ISBN 978-1-5108-6911-0

CURRAN ASSOCIATES INC.
proceedings.com